The Flying Scots

A CENTURY OF AVIATION IN SCOTLAND

Jack Webster

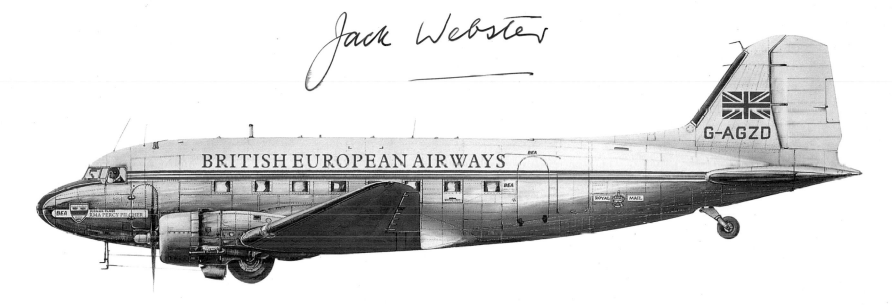

Douglas DC-3 Pionair Class Dakota G–AGZD "RMA Percy Pilcher"

The British European Airways fleet of DC-3s was modernised by Scottish Aviation at Prestwick in the early 1950s and converted to 32 seat configuration. As such the aircraft were known as the 'Pionair' Class and named after British pioneers in aviation. They remained in service with BEA until 1962.

BY JACK WEBSTER

PUBLISHED BY

FOREWORD BY AIR VICE-MARSHAL SANDY JOHNSTONE

PAINTINGS BY DUGALD CAMERON

THE GLASGOW ROYAL CONCERT HALL

The copyright © for the articles in this book belongs to Jack Webster

Photographs: © Aberdeen Press & Journal; © Ian Allan Library; © Bill Bell; © Bond Helicopters Ltd; © Brian Boyle; © Dugald Cameron; © Alan Carlaw; © Peter Clegg; © Aird Crooks; © Rick Brewell & Mark Hipkin, MOD, Crown copyright; © Iain Duffy; © J D Ferguson; © R M Gibson; © Glasgow Museum of Transport; © The Herald; © Jetstream Aircraft Ltd; © Ian Johnston; © John King; © Gordon McAdie; © The Mitchell Library, Glasgow; © David Reid; © Eric Starling; © Strathclyde Regional Archives; © John Stroud; © Scottish Records Office; © Wilf White

First published in Great Britain in 1994 by
The Glasgow Royal Concert Hall
2 Sauchiehall Street
Glasgow G2 3NY

ISBN 0 9522174 2 2

A catalogue record for this book is available from the British Library

Design and production by Alan Carlaw

Typeset by Squadron Prints Ltd, Giffnock, Glasgow
Printed by Elpeeko Ltd, Lincoln

Contents

Erratum

Page 7, last paragraph, line 8 Nothing detracts from the genius of the Wright brothers, Orville and Wilbur, who came through to take their place in aviation history in 1903 as the *first people to fly in a heavier-than-air machine.*
Page 38, caption – Charcoal portrait of Archie McKellar when he was with 605 Squadron

Subjects selected by Jack Webster, Ken Colville, Dugald Cameron & Alan Carlaw
Cover and other paintings by Dugald Cameron
Front cover – Percy Pilcher, Britain's first aeronaut, making an early flight at Cardross in the Bat Mk.2 glider in June 1895
Rear cover – Prestwick designed and built, a Jetstream 41 for Impulse Airlines of Australia over Turnberry in July 1994

Foreword
by
Air Vice-Marshal Sandy Johnstone CB DFC AE DL RAF (Retd)

Scotland is a proud nation, and justifiably so, for it has so much of which to be proud, not least in its contribution to the world of aviation throughout the past century.

In an age when science has made such remarkable strides that one now accepts space travel as an everyday occurrence, it is all too easy to forget the great achievements of the bygone days which laid the foundation for this remarkable transformation. Apart from the sterling efforts of its early designers and manufacturers of heavier-than-air machines, Scotland's aviation history is riddled with great milestones – many now forgotten – which have played a significant role in the development of aviation worldwide. How many, for instance, remember that RAF Leuchars, the famous Royal Air Force base in the Kingdom of Fife, is among the oldest military flying stations in the world, having maintained, non-stop, an operational role since first being used by the Army in 1908 as a testing ground for man-lifting kites. Today, of course, it continues to perform its vital role in the air defence of the realm. Nor, as a further example, should it ever be forgotten that two great Scots, the Marquess of Douglas and Clydesdale (later Duke of Hamilton) and David McIntyre were the first men ever to conquer Mount Everest during their epic flight in 1933. The list goes on and on.

We must congratulate The Glasgow Royal Concert Hall for initiating the trilogy "Trains and Boats and Planes", as all three volumes are packed with valuable and interesting historical data about Scotland's invaluable contributions on the sea, on the land and in the air, all written in such delightful and informative style that they are a real pleasure to read, at the same time helping to re-kindle one's burning feelings of pride in the countless achievements which have helped to keep Scotland the proud nation it has always been. What a boon it would be if these three volumes were made compulsory reading for the Scottish youth of today!

Spitfire IA flown by Sqn Ldr Sandy Johnstone when Commanding Officer of No. 602 Squadron during the Battle of Britain

AUTHOR'S NOTE

Given the inventive genius of the Scots, you could have been sure they wouldn't be far away when such a prospect as flying came within the reach of human experience.

In many a blissful dream we have flapped our arms and gained a sense of levitation. But ambitious Scots have been trying to turn that fantasy into a reality for nearly 500 years.

In more practical terms they have been engaged in it since the tail-end of the 19th century, when a Glasgow naval architect, Percy Pilcher, came close to snatching the glory which fell instead to the Wright brothers of America, the first people to fly a heavier-than-air machine.

Since then the Scots have been much nearer to the heart of aviation than most of us realise. From the planes and airships of Beardmore's and the whirlybirds from Weir's of Cathcart to the high technology of Ferranti, the exquisite aero engines of Rolls-Royce and the modern success of Jetstream production at Prestwick, the contribution of such a small nation has been staggering.

But even the technology has to make way for a deeply moving story of human courage and endeavour, involving names like Jim Mollison, Archie McKellar, David McIntyre and the Duke of Hamilton.

Into a century of aviation in Scotland come heroic figures like Lady MacRobert of Douneside in Aberdeenshire, who had her own answer to Hitler when she suffered unthinkable personal tragedy.

And the Fuhrer's own deputy, Rudolf Hess, cannot be ignored for that most bizarre episode of the Second World War, when he suddenly appeared over Scotland, crash-landing his plane near Eaglesham and bringing his own eccentric solution to that war with Germany.

In starting out by wondering if there really is a book to be written about Scotland's part in the comparatively short history of flying, you are soon overwhelmed by the magnitude of the task. How can you do even faint justice to such a story?

It has been no less than breathtaking to uncover the truth about The Flying Scots. Here we have something to sing about, which prompts me to echo Frank Sinatra's invitation: *Come Fly With Me* – and share the surprise.

The author and publisher would like to thank Dugald Cameron for his historical research

PERCY PILCHER

The notion that we minor mortals could somehow gain the freedom of birds in the sky and take flight has long been a dream of human imagination. As far back as 1507 a chap called John Damian was fitting himself with wings made from the feathers of a hen and attempting to fly by jumping from the ramparts of Stirling Castle.

By the grace of God he survived, cursing himself for not having had the sense to use eagles' feathers!

In 1784 another adventurer, James Tytler, became Scotland's first "floater" when he rose in a hot-air balloon from Comely Bank in Edinburgh, while in 1815 the English balloonist James Sadler flew from Glasgow to Milngavie.

John Damian

Coming much closer to the reality of raising a manned machine into the air, a lecturer in naval architecture at Glasgow University might well have gained the lasting fame which went instead to the Wright brothers of America.

Sadly, Percy Sinclair Pilcher, brilliant innovator and personable young man, was killed in 1899 at the age of thirty-two, on a wet and windy day when he decided to demonstrate his latest glider rather than disappoint the assembled spectators.

Pilcher, who was exactly the same age as Wilbur Wright, carried out experiments at his lodgings in Byres Road, Glasgow, but had built half a dozen machines and was close to powered flight when the Wrights were just building their first glider. No wonder a poet wrote of Pilcher:

> How great a game of chance, how close to fame
> Yet few are those who now recall your name
> Or what your courage meant.

It was a case of what-might-have-been for this son of a Scots lady, born in Bath in 1867 but orphaned by the time he was ten. Entering the Navy at the age of thirteen, he sailed the seas till he was twenty. He then returned to his mother's homeland and was apprenticed in the engineering department of Elder's shipyard in Govan, which later became Fairfield's. As a young draughtsman he made a deep impression upon those around him with his sharp, inventive mind.

By the early 1890s Percy Pilcher had become assistant to Sir John Biles,

Percy Pilcher, 1867–1899

James Tytler's 'fire' balloon

Vincenzo Lunardi, a flamboyant young Italian balloonist, demonstrated his craft to Glaswegians on 23 November 1785 when he rose from St Andrew's Square watched by a crowd of around 100,000 people. The weather was fine as Lunardi 'ascended into the atmosphere with majestic grandeur, to the astonishment and admiration of the spectators'. The balloon passed over Hamilton and Lanark before making a good landing near Hawick. The 110 mile journey had taken two and a half hours. A second ascent a few weeks later began with a near calamity when a dissenting preacher known as 'Lothian Tam' got tangled with the mooring ropes and was lifted 20 feet into the air before being released and falling to the ground without serious injury.

professor of naval architecture and marine engineering at Glasgow University, as well as a draughtsman at the Clydebank shipyard which became John Brown's.

With a developing interest in flying, he took out patents which included one for "captive balloons, kites etc." He became particularly caught up in the world of the German Otto Lilienthal and his first successful piloted glider flight in 1891. With the help of his sister Ella, Pilcher built his first full-size glider, the Bat, at his Byres Road lodgings.

In 1895 he went to Germany to visit Lilienthal and was given the chance to fly successfully in the German's glider. Back in Scotland, he tried out his Bat at the farms of Wallacetown and Auchensail near Cardross, Dunbartonshire, with that method of launching which was to run downhill against the wind and take short jumps, the kind of thing which can amuse in jerky old newsreels.

Then came the tragic news that Lilienthal had been killed while flying one of his gliders, leaving Percy Pilcher as perhaps the leading aviator in the world at that time.

Now heading towards the break-through of powered flight, Pilcher had moved from Glasgow to Kent, where he developed his most successful glider, the Hawk. Having agreed to demonstrate it at the Stamford Hall seat of Lord Braye on 30 September 1899, he defied the weather for the sake of the onlookers. But a structural failure sent him crashing to the ground. Still alive when taken from the wreckage, he died two days later, still only thirty-two. Nothing detracts from the genius of the Wright brothers, Orville and Wilbur, who came through to take their place in aviation history in 1903 as the It is simply that there is no glory for those who failed to make it, even if they were denied only by death. But Scotland has good reason at least to remember the name of Percy Pilcher, the outstanding young man who gave that first thrust towards a century of aviation in Scotland.

Pilcher with the Bat Mk.3 at Auchensail in 1895

His third glider, the Gull

The Beetle, Pilcher's second glider, at Auchensail in 1895

Percy & Ella demonstrate the Bat's portability at Wallacetown Farm

An early photograph of Pilcher with the Bat glider as originally built without the horizontal tail

Pilcher's fourth glider, the Hawk, was built in Glasgow but not flown in Scotland. Seen here in the grounds of Glasgow University

To Percy Pilcher

By Philip Jarrett
19 April, 1983

Youthful dreams of flight, nurtured in your heart,
Matured as you matured; became a part
Of ev'ry waking day.
And pensive hours on landlost, windswept seas,
Where graceful, long-winged seabirds soared with ease,
Helped guide you on your way.

Then came the day you built your fledgling wings
Of bamboo, wire, and fabric — fragile things
On which life would rely.
A pilgrimage to Berlin followed now,
Where Master Lilienthal showed you how
To trespass in the sky.

In pioneering steps the work progressed,
Bat, clumsy Beetle, Gull, and then the best;
The light and sturdy Hawk.
Towed aloft by gently plodding horses
To vie with Nature's sly and unseen forces:
An airborne, bobbing cork.

Tough yet athletic, soon you learned the way
To hold control within your body's sway
And make the sky your own.
To longer flights your airy dreams then soared,
And with the help of businessman and lord
Your new machine was grown.

But ere the test of powered wings began,
A hasty, ill-timed flight upset the plan
To which you'd given birth.
Death's evil sirens did your soul entice
To make the last and greatest sacrifice;
Then cast you to the earth.

How great a game of chance, how close to fame,
Yet few are those who now recall your name
Or what your courage meant.
The lonely grave in Brompton where you lie
Grows mossy underneath a mocking sky:
A short life bravely spent.

But those who now traverse the lofty ways
In these jet-powered, ocean-spanning days
Cast hist'ry in their wake.
You knew this time would come, and played your part
In teaching Man a new and wond'rous art:
And gave life for its sake.

Pilcher in flight – probably the first photograph of a heavier-than-air machine in flight

8

SCOTLAND'S FIRST AIRCRAFT

With the success of America's Orville and Wilbur Wright in showing the way to the skies in 1903 - and France's Louis Bleriot making the first air crossing of the English Channel in 1909 - the craze for flying was spreading like wildfire across the world.

With its fine reputation for engineering, inventiveness and generally bright ideas, Scotland was never very far out of the pioneering picture. If America had the Wright brothers, Scotland could produce the three Barnwell brothers, Frank and Harold from Balfron, near Stirling, who would make their own contribution to the development of aviation.

Their father was managing director of the Fairfield shipyard in Glasgow and it was on the lawn of the family home at Elcho House, Balfron, that Harold first experimented with model gliders. By now he and Frank were completely caught up in the possibilities of flying.

Frank Barnwell, who was born in 1880, followed his years at Fettes College with an apprenticeship at his father's shipyard but sandwiched that with a degree in naval architecture at Glasgow University.

Having gone to America, he actually met the Wright brothers but returned to join Harold and another brother, Archibald, in the family business of the Grampian Motor and Engineering Company at Causewayhead, Stirling.

There was much excitement in the area when it was learned that the Barnwell brothers were quietly building an aeroplane. The first trial was set for a December day of 1908, in a field at Cornton Farm, Causewayhead, but they failed to give their machine the necessary power for a 35-mile-per-hour take off.

Instead the Barnwells turned their attention to building a biplane and its debut of July 1909 was described by the Stirling Journal: "When the engine was started the aeroplane, like some huge white-winged bird, rushed forward and with a rapid sweep rose into the air. The nose was pointed at a very high angle and after travelling about 80 yards the machine suddenly dipped and came rushing to the ground.

"Although the aeroplane was badly damaged, Mr Barnwell escaped with a few slight cuts and bruises and was highly delighted with the results."

That plane was repaired but the Barnwells built a water cooled, twin cylinder engine at their Grampian works and fitted it to a monoplane, in which Harold flew 600 yards at a height of 50ft. Though that 1911 adventure ended upside down in a ploughed field, he persevered with this plane and reached the success of a five-mile flight at a height of 200ft. In 1911, he also won the J R K Law prize for the first half-mile flight in an all-Scottish aeroplane.

Harold gained his pilot's certificate at Brooklands and went on to be the

The Barnwell biplane of 1909 at Causewayhead, Stirling

highly-regarded chief test pilot and instructor at Vickers. He died in 1917, when his plane crashed in circumstances which suggested he had taken ill at the controls. Brother Frank became chief designer at the Bristol Aeroplane Company but, in a familiar pattern of pioneering, was killed in 1938 when testing an aircraft of his own creation.

Barnwell monoplane won the J R K Law Prize in 1911

Gibson's No.II built at Leith in 1910

That pioneering spirit was everywhere in Scotland at that time. At his motor engineering and coachbuilding premises in Leith, John Gibson and his son George were building their first plane in 1909 and went on to produce ten more, exhibiting one of them at the Scottish International Exhibition of 1911. In the approach to the First World War, the Gibsons were building a machine of 40ft wingspan but the war brought their efforts to an end for good.

In Dundee, a man called Preston Watson began his plane-building in 1903, met with mixed fortunes and finally lost his life while serving with the Royal Naval Air Service in 1915. A Rothesay blacksmith, Mr A.B.Baird, was among a variety

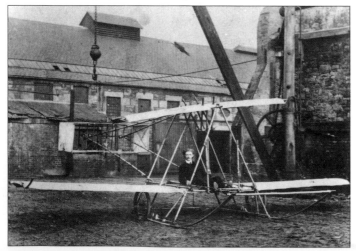

The Preston Watson No.1 of 1909

of other Scots who managed to build themselves an aeroplane though not all of them, it has to be said, actually took to the air!

As a measure of the public interest, however, the Scottish Aeronautical Society organised an international aviation meeting which drew a crowd of 200,000 people to the racecourse at Lanark in 1910. At the International Exhibition a year later, the exhibits on view included Percy Pilcher's glider, the Hawk, which had been lent by the Royal Scottish Museum in Edinburgh.

A Scottish Aviation Company was formed to provide machines and train pilots and two flying schools sprang up at Lanark and Barrhead in 1911, though neither survived for long. That early enthusiasm for the new craze had passed before the First World War but there were still interesting developments.

The head of the experimental tank at Denny's shipyard in Dumbarton, E.R.Mumford, turned his hand to air propellers in 1905 and the result, a few years later, was the Denny-Mumford helicopter. Once again, the First World War took the sting out of that kind of enterprise and nothing more came of it.

In another development in Scotland, Peter Burt of the Acme Wringer Company patented the single sleeve-valve engine in 1909 and it was put into practice by the Argyll Motor Company of Alexandria. That company went into liquidation and,

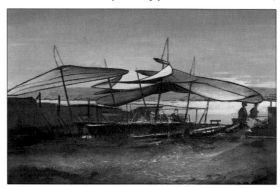

The Denny-Mumford helicopter in its final form with floats (1905–1914)

although Burt continued his work, the patents were sold to America.

After the war, Burt's idea of an engine appeared in aircraft of the Bristol Aeroplane Company but the full development, which Bristol shared with the Air Ministry, had cost a staggering £2 million.

Dunne D1 glider at Glen Tilt, Blair Athol in 1907 and the D4 powered aircraft of 1908

AVIATION AT BEARDMORE'S

The family firm of Beardmore was best known in the 19th century for its Parkhead Forge in the east end of Glasgow, providing much employment in the production of heavy forgings and armour plate.

But perhaps the most dramatic episode in the firm's history was its venture into the building of aeroplanes and airships in the early part of the 20th century.

The credit for this remarkable story goes to William Beardmore, born in 1856, educated at Ayr Academy and Glasgow High School and apprenticed into the family forge at the age of fourteen. Once he assumed control of the business he displayed an ingenuity and enthusiasm which brought work to more than 42,000 people on Clydeside.

The first major move came in 1906 when, following the trend of bigger shipyards, he went down river to Dalmuir, near Clydebank, and built the biggest yard on the Clyde. Soon he was diversifying into everything from battleships to airships, locomotives to flying boats, beyond the scale of any other company in Britain. He struck the peak period of shipbuilding but within 25 years the whole adventure had come to an end.

As Ian Johnston wrote in his splendid book about the company: "The closure of Beardmore's great yard after a relatively brief working life says as much about the fickle impermanence of human activity, no matter how sound, as it does about dismal financial performance."

Because William Beardmore had some wonderful ideas, ahead of his time,

and deserved a better fate for his enterprise. Instead, he was finally removed from the board and ended life, with the title of Lord Invernairn, at his Highland home near Loch Ness, where he died in 1936 at the age of eighty.

Combining the interest in ships and his newer fascination with flying, Beardmore had tried to interest the Admiralty, as early as 1912, in something called a Hydroplane Carrier, which was the forerunner of the aircraft carrier. The outbreak of the First World War brought a more prompt response, with the need for shipbuilders and engineers to adapt to the building of aeroplanes as well, under the control of another distinguished Scot, Lord Weir, who was appointed Director of Munitions in Scotland in 1915.

Again with his foresight, William Beardmore had already secured the British manufacturing rights of the German DFW biplane. At the same time he had gained the rights for the Austro Daimler 120hp aero engine.

Large sheds for the building of aircraft were erected at Dalmuir and the Beardmore DFW seaplane went into production for the Royal Naval Air Service.

The company set up an office to produce original aircraft designs and followed through to build some prototypes. Remarkably during that first war, no fewer than 487 aircraft and twelve kite balloons were made at Dalmuir, on top of the repair and experimental work and production of spare parts.

The first Beardmore built BE2c, No.1099, at Dalmuir in February 1915

The Dalmuir Works with BE2cs under construction

Planes were taken to the nearby Robertson Park where the wings were fitted to the fuselage and the completed craft then took off from a grass field and were flown across to the aerodromes at Renfrew or Inchinnan. Seaplanes, which were popular at that time, were simply lowered into the Clyde by crane. By the end of that war, Beardmore's aviation department was capable of building six large aircraft, 20 medium and 15 small ones at the same time.

Before the First War, William Beardmore had also cottoned on to the

Beardmore WB I as built with 'N' struts

possibility of airships and had applied for patents. With his first order, he began building them in the seaplane shed at Dalmuir but soon moved across river to put up a massive airship shed at Inchinnan.

With much public excitement about this form of transport, Beardmore built Airship No 24, which had its maiden flight from Inchinnan in July 1917. During the war a German airship was brought down on the Essex coast and, when examined, was found to be so superior that its type was copied. So Beardmore was given the task of building one of the new class, R34, the model which made history in 1919 when it was the first aircraft to fly the Atlantic both ways.

Though the end of the First World War signalled an end to aircraft production in Britain, Beardmore kept open his design office and foresaw a bright future for the flying machine. The company catalogue told of new designs and and of the determination to build Beardmore planes fitted with their own engines.

In 1920 it started the first scheduled air service from Glasgow to London (actually from Renfrew to the Croydon Aerodrome associated with so much Biggles-type fiction),

A Dukinfield Jones (test pilot) and G Tilghman Richards (chief designer) with the WB I

mainly to demonstrate the possibilities. The Beardmore vision was very much on the right lines but the general enthusiasm waned after the war and, with the Scots company running into financial difficulties, the aviation department was closed.

At the end of the war there had been a feeling that Clydeside might well develop a role in airships similar to that of the water variety. Beardmore and Cunard were among the companies meeting in London to discuss a network of overseas routes for airships, including a transatlantic service

Beardmore WB V at the Isle of Grain in December 1917

With the likely development of the aeroplane, however, there were soon

The R34 was the last rigid airship to be used by the Admiralty seen here at its birthplace, Inchinnan

Beardmore WB X G–EAQJ at Renfrew in 1920

The WB XXVI fighter aircraft for Latvia

forecasts that airships would become obsolete before long. Though bigger craft were produced, the whole sorry tale of airships came to an end in 1930 when the R101 crashed on a French hillside, burst into flames and killed most of those on board. Sadly, the engine of the ill-fated airship was pioneered at Beardmore's of Parkhead.

With encouragement from the Air Ministry, the aviation department was re-opened in 1924 and W S Shackleton became the chief designer at Dalmuir.

Beardmore had acquired the rights to a system of aircraft construction created by Dr Adolph Rohrbach, who had worked for the Zeppelin Staaken company. Dr Rohrbach was the man who developed all-metal, stressed-skin construction, producing the design which laid the foundation of the modern aeroplane. At

The 'Wee Bee' G–EBJJ at Lympne in 1924

Beardmore built Wight 840 seaplane No.1401 at Dalmuir

The R36 Airship at Inchinnan

Dalmuir they built his 160ft-wingspan plane called the Inflexible, the largest span of anything built in Britain until the Bristol Brabazon of 1953. They also designed and built the "Wee Bee" ultra-light aircraft which won the Air Ministry competition at Lympne in 1924.

In that pioneering period, Beardmore also became involved in the novel plan of Glasgow engineer George Bennie, who thought he could cut the journey from Glasgow to Edinburgh to twenty minutes with his railplane. Beardmore built the passenger car like an aircraft fuselage and an experimental track was built over the railway line at Milngavie.

Bennie's Railplane ran first on 4 July 1930 but came to nothing. By then Beardmore's aviation department had closed for good.

It had all been a great adventure while it lasted. And William Beardmore must remain among those wonderfully imaginative and inventive Scots who could always make things happen, successfully or otherwise.

Beardmore 'Inflexible', J7557

The second 'Inverness' flying boat N184 built by Beardmore in 1929

THE RAF'S FOUNDING FATHERS

Though the name of Hugh Trenchard is generally given as "Father of the Royal Air Force," that credit must be challenged on behalf of two distinguished Scots who really had more to do with it than Trenchard.

One is David Henderson, son of a Glasgow shipbuilder and engineer, who reached the heights in the Army before fighting official opposition to establish the new flying service in Britain.

The other is William Weir, from the famous Glasgow engineering works at Cathcart (he was a great favourite with Lloyd George and Winston Churchill), who became Secretary of State for Air at the inception of the RAF - and had to persuade a reluctant Trenchard to take on the leading role in the post-war service.

The much-neglected story of David Henderson in particular deserves attention. Born in 1862 and having studied engineering under Lord Kelvin at Glasgow University, Henderson chose an army career, joined the Argyll and Sutherland Highlanders and was later at the Battle of Omdurman.

By the time of the Boer War he was Director of Military Intelligence, under Lord Kitchener, enlarging the network of spies. Wounded and much decorated, he began to write books on what he had learned. He had also become a popular and well-rounded man, pianist and composer, designer of theatrical sets and the one who set Kipling's poems to music.

A Brigadier by 1908 and always keen on new ideas, Henderson was intrigued by the flying achievements of the Wright brothers. He began to think of aeroplanes as fighting machines but found no enthusiasm in government or military circles, the army taking the view that they would frighten the horses!

Under an assumed name, Henderson learned to fly and became a pilot at the age of forty-nine, when he was described as "a born flyer." Despite official coolness, however, the Government did ask a defence committee to consider

David Henderson

the future of air power and Henderson was in the three-man team which gave the technical report.

It was the work of that team which brought the formation of an air service in Britain. The Royal Flying Corps came into existence in 1912, when they had to decide on the size of a "squadron" - and even on the word itself

Henderson was appointed Director of Military Training at the War Office, still with a special interest in the development of flying. That made him responsible for training the British Army which would cross to France in 1914. His real work for the Royal Flying Corps, however, began with his appointment as Director-General of Military Aeronautics.

Four days after the start of the First World War the new RFC gathered at Dover, one squadron having flown south from Montrose. As forty-one planes crossed to France on the first day, it was worth contemplating that only five years had passed since Louis Bleriot made the first-ever flight across the Channel.

Henderson went over to be their commander in the field, by now having been knighted. Meanwhile Colonel Trenchard was given the task of building up a force from what was left back home.

Sir John French, commander of the British Forces, was soon reporting from the front that Henderson and his flying machines were giving invaluable service, not only with reconnaissance and information but through fighting in the air. From those beginnings of 1912 the Royal Flying Corps had grown so rapidly that Henderson decided he had to get back to his desk, handing over command in the field to Hugh Trenchard. The forthright Scot, who had gathered himself some enemies in Press and Parliament, then reported to General Smuts, the famous Boer leader who had been asked to examine our defence arrangements. Henderson had a proposal: To form one complete air service, administered by a single air ministry.

Lord Rothermere became president of the Air Council, with Henderson and Trenchard under him, but neither could agree with Rothermere's policies and both resigned, ironically, on 1 April 1918, the very day on which the Royal Air Force came into being

Rothermere himself decided to resign - and that was how William Weir of Glasgow came into the picture. Weir's family firm not only built many complete aircraft for the war, refusing to take any profit on such work, but later took up the development of the autogyro, which led to the helicopter as we know it.

The Weirs also had the foresight to give financial backing to Frank Whittle when others wouldn't support his idea of a jet engine.

Because of Churchill's high regard for William Weir, he put him in charge

William Weir

Beardmore built Sopwith 2F-1 Camel based at Turnhouse and embarked in HMS Furious making
a successful bambing attack on the Tondern airship sheds on 19 July 1918 after flying off in the North Sea.
This was the first attack on a land target made by carrier-based aircraft

of aircraft production. So when Lord Rothermere resigned, he became Secretary of State for Air and was soon raised to the peerage as Lord Weir of Eastwood.

All this was achieved by the time he was forty-one, the more remarkable because he was a comparatively little-known figure with no standing in politics. But Churchill knew he was the man for the job - and that he was dedicated to the notion of independent air power.

Yet one of Weir's first tasks was to persuade Hugh Trenchard to take charge of the RAF. The latter could be awkward and arrogant and was spending much of his time just sitting on a bench in London's Green Park. Behind all this, however, William Weir detected qualities that would make Trenchard the man he wanted for the job. Finally he made it plain he was issuing an order which could not be disobeyed.

So that was the curious introduction to the post which would later gain Trenchard his title as "Father of the Royal Air Force."

Meanwhile, David Henderson returned to the army, soon encountering the tragedy of his son's death in a flying accident at Turnberry. Nevertheless he took part in the peace talks of 1919 and became head of the new League of Red Cross Societies in Geneva.

But he had driven himself hard. When he died at the age of fifty-nine, his ashes were buried at Girvan. The Times called him "The Maker of the RAF." Even Lord Trenchard himself paid tribute to the vision of David Henderson who, along with Lord Weir, surely played the most significant role in creating the Royal Air Force.

THE TURNBERRY TALE

The idyllic setting of Turnberry Hotel, overlooking the Firth of Clyde with its golf courses sweeping down to a rugged coastline, is well known to an international clientele, not least to those who follow the Open Championship to that popular corner of Ayrshire.

But few who praise its charms would credit the devastation which fell upon those picturesque greens and fairways during the two world wars.

Turnberry was just establishing itself on the golfing map when it was taken over as a training centre for pilots of the Royal Flying Corps and other Commonwealth units during the 1914-18 war. To complete the requisitioning, the hotel became an officers' mess, especially for Canadians.

The monument on the hill above the 12th green is a memorial to those Turnberry pilots who lost their lives in the war.

But if Turnberry's golf was interrupted by the First World War it was nothing to what happened in the Second. Though professional pilots had declared it unsuitable as a modern airfield, it became one nevertheless.

As RAF Coastal Command prepared to move in, big machines levelled out the undulations, laid acres of concrete and tarmacadam and built hangars and huts in time for the Liberators and Beaufighters which would use Turnberry as a base for pursuing U-boats and dropping depth charges.

That conversion to an airfield seemed to have ruined Turnberry's future as a golfing centre. But the vision and determination of the British Transport Hotel chairman, Frank Hole, sparked off a truly remarkable restoration.

Runways had to be uprooted and new contours created in a massive operation to give back beauty and golfing glory to Turnberry. The Ailsa course re-opened in 1951 and staged its first Open Championship in 1977.

As Turnberry headed for a world-wide reputation, few would have believed that such a golfing phoenix could have arisen from the ashes of a wartime airfield.

Bristol M1C at Turnberry during WWI

A Bristol Fighter awaits take off c.1917

THE FLYING CLUBS

Pilots coming back from the First World War brought with them an enthusiasm to extend their activities into peacetime flying clubs. Five such men used to meet for morning coffee in Miss Cranston's Tearoom in the centre of Glasgow and out of their discussions came the idea of forming a Scottish Flying Club.

Local business giants like Lord Weir, Sir Harold Yarrow and Sir Maurice Denny were among those who put up the initial £2000 and the club came into being in November 1927, with a single-bay hangar at Renfrew Airport. They bought one Cirrus Moth and were loaned another by Mr J G Weir.

Whatever the original intentions, this was not just a matter of hobby flying. By 1933 the Scottish Flying Club had a five-year lease of the entire aerodrome and had agreed to run it for Renfrew Town Council. It also took on air traffic control and, with aviation on the up-and-up, was soon handling 30 passenger planes every day during the summer.

The club was there to encourage flying and by 1939 it had 210 pilot members and 320 associates, the pilots including distinguished names like the Marquis of Clydesdale, George Pinkerton, Archie McKellar and Gibby Rae, who all find their place in this book.

The club trained many first-class women pilots, including Winifred Drinkwater (later Mrs Short of flying-boat fame) who proved an outstanding pupil and a substantial winner of trophies. She also gained an engineer's licence before the age when she legally could hold it.

Jock Houston became chief instructor in the early 1930s but sadly was killed in 1937 while a passenger in a plane being demonstrated.

At the outbreak of war in 1939 the Air Ministry requisitioned Renfrew Aerodrome and 60 members were off to be wartime flyers. Of those, no fewer than 18 were killed as pilots with the RAF.

The story of the Scottish Flying Club after the war was far from satisfactory. Renfrew became a state airport in 1946 and, in that bleak period of austerity and nationalisation, the club was given notice to quit, poor and insensitive reward not only for wartime service and sacrifice but for all the energy, skill and money put into building it up.

The owners of Perth Aerodrome at Scone heard of the plight and invited them to fly from there instead, an arrangement which continued until 1952 when fresh approaches to the Government Minister involved (he happened to be the West Renfrewshire MP, John S. Maclay) gained them a return to Renfrew. By then, however, the splendid premises they had created in 1934 had become the civil terminal for the airport.

The identity of the Scottish Flying Club eventually disappeared, merged into

Early days of the Scottish flying Club. DH 60 Moth, G–AAJL, at Renfrew c.1930 with Arkleston Cemetry in the background

the Scottish Aero Club at Scone, which was still operating into the 1990s .

The club also bought Couplaw Farm at Strathaven, providing facilities for other bodies like the West of Scotland Flying Club and the Clydesdale Flying Club as well as the Universities' Gliding Club.

But the spirit of the flying club movement remained strong, as demonstrated on Tayside. As the in-between city, not favoured with an airport like Glasgow, Edinburgh and Aberdeen, Dundee nevertheless built Riverside Airstrip in the mid-1960s, on the suggestion of Willie Logan, whose company was then building the Tay Road Bridge.

Despite its existence, however, all attempts to form a local flying club came unstuck. Then a local businessman and aviation enthusiast, Lovat Fraser, suggested to two fellow gliding instructors, Alistair Gillespie and Douglas Shearer, that they should form a company called Aerosport and hire out a plane. They acquired a machine called a Nipper and could joke about its appearance ("Short stubby wings sprouting from a short dumpy fuselage, an undercarriage worked with rubber bands and a cockpit so small that the pilot had to tuck his elbows into the wing roots!"). But it gave great service and was hired out at £4 an hour.

Tayside Flying Club at Dundee showing some of the Cessna and Piper aircraft beside the clubhouse in 1993

Alan Chapman's Piper Cherokee G–ARVT and the West of Scotland Flying Club's Rallye Commodore 180 G–AXIT at Glenforsa Airfield, Mull in 1972

Aerosport's first aircraft – Slingsby T.66 Nipper 3 G-AVXD overflies the Tay on approach to Dundee.

Tayside Flying Club's Beagle 121 Pup 1, G–AWKM

To comply with the laws on flying training, they had to form a flying club but the commercial development continued, now under the name of Tayside Aviation Ltd.

In 1982 a new hangar was provided by the Scottish Development Agency and the company became involved in aircraft maintenance and repairs. In 1987 it spread to Aberdeen Airport where it offered flying training and started a flying club. In 1990 the Hong Kong Government asked Tayside Aviation to train cadet pilots for its Air Force and in 1994 our own Ministry of Defence placed a £3 million contract to train 500 air cadets per year.

Tayside Aviation had therefore become a thoroughly healthy enterprise involving, between Dundee and Aberdeen, 35 full-time and 20 part-time employees. The concept of the flying club in Scotland, generated over a cup of coffee in Glasgow after the First World War, had survived towards a new century.

And with it went the enthusiasm for gliding as symbolised by the Scottish Gliding Union, which Andrew Thorburn of Kirkcaldy began in 1934 and which has found its home mainly in Fife, where the soaring conditions around the Lomond Hills have proved irresistible. Among the many achievements, one of its members, George Lee, who was a fighter pilot in the RAF, had the unequalled record of winning the World Gliding Championship three times in a row.

Andrew Thorburn in a Falcon I glider at Bishop Hill near Kinross in 1937

Flt Lt George Lee, a pilot with 43 Squadron at Leuchars in the late 1970s, with his glider and Phantom jet

The Scottish Gliding Union in 1991 at Portmoak

Tayside's Cessna FA.152 Aerobat G–TFCI at Dundee

THE WEIR AUTOGYROS

The famous Glasgow engineering firm, Weir's of Cathcart, was among many large companies in Britain turning to the most unexpected products in the emergency of the First World War.

But who would have foreseen that the company which had become best known for supplying pumps to the ships of the world would produce or be responsible for 1100 aeroplanes for the 1914-18 conflict?

An even more dramatic involvement with flying machines, however, came after the First War when Weir's was to be found in the forefront of developing the autogyro, which led to the helicopter as we know it today.

The word "helicopter" was already in existence, describing a machine with power-driven rotors which both lifted it and drove it forward. The trouble was that, if the engine failed, the rotors would stop and the helicopter would crash.

All that was changed by a Spanish aristocrat called Juan de la Cierva who, with family money behind him, came up with an ingenious invention called the Autogyro, the first rotating-wing aircraft capable of controlled flight. Cierva's idea was to propel his machine, like a fixed wing aircraft, by engine-driven screws but to lift it by rotors which were driven by the airflow created by the aircraft's motion. This meant that, if the engine failed, the free-rotor would still revolve and bring the machine more gently to the ground. In other words, it was safer.

Cierva brought his invention for demonstration at Farnborough in 1925 and among the spectators intrigued by his idea was James G Weir, of the Glasgow engineering family. His brother William (Lord Weir) wrote on 21 October 1925: "Jimmy rang me up to say he had been at Farnborough to see the performance of the new Autogyro aeroplane....In Jimmy's opinion, it marks the real beginning of aviation, apart from its war importance."

Out of that, James G Weir found the finance and became chairman of the Cierva Autogyro Company, which didn't build the machines but carried out research and development so that patents could be acquired. Among the manufacturers who gained licences to build the Autogyro was G and J Weir of Cathcart.

James G Weir CMG CBE
1887 – 1973

Air Cdre James Weir's Cierva autogyro
at Renfrew around 1928

Lord Weir became so caught up in the idea brought home by his brother that he wrote to Henry Ford in 1928, obviously trying to interest him in mass production. He was glad to tell Ford that these machines could now be built with as much safety as the motor car – and required no more manipulative skill.

Henry Ford's son Edsel turned him down and Lord Weir was later to write that "the development quite naturally met with lukewarm and half-hearted support and encouragement from all authority and even from the scientific world. Such is the normal history of all great inventions."

The Weirs were far-sighted men. The family firm, as opposed to James Weir himself, didn't become financially involved with the Autogyro project until 1932, by which time Cierva's affairs had reached crisis point.

Coming at the depth of the Depression, when Weir's was being dragged down by the slump in shipbuilding, it tells much about the Cathcart company that, at that point, it was prepared to acquire rights of development, including the pursuit of an Autogyro engine of its own design.

Weir produced its first Autogyro in 1933, a single-seater with a fuselage only 15ft long, fitted with two rotor blades sweeping a circle of 28ft in diameter. The design was started under F L Hodgess and the Douglas Dryad engine was the result of C G Pullin coming to Weir's from Douglas Motors Ltd. He was joined by a former Douglas colleague, Mickey Walker, who became involved in the design of Weir aero engines.

The second Weir Autogyro had its engine built at Cathcart and was first

Weir W-1 Autogyro, 1933

Weir W-2 Autogyro, 1934

Weir W-3 Autogyro, 1936

Weir W-4 Autogyro, 1937

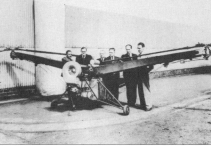

Weir W-5 helicopter, at Cathcart in 1938
F L Hodgess, Dr J A J Bennett, C G Pullin,
R F Bowyer, G E Walker, K Watson

The Kay Gyroplane on display at the Glasgow Museum of Transport

tested at Abbotsinch in 1934. Improved versions continued to appear through 1936, the year in which, by a sad irony, the creative Cierva was killed when an airliner crashed at Croydon Aerodrome.

The Weir team was now producing an Autogyro which could jump straight up from the ground, a revolutionary step forward which proved to be the starting point for solving the age-old problem which had bedevilled the creation of a safe and viable helicopter.

Weir's had broken through to the machine of the future and the team which produced the first Weir helicopter deserves to be recorded: Dr J A J Bennett, C G Pullin, K Watson, G E Walker, F L Hodgess, R F Bowyer, T Nesbitt, L Pullin, Wm Stein and R A Pullin (eldest son of C G) who was also the pilot when initial trials took place at Dalrymple in Ayrshire in June 1938.

For an invention which would play such a part in Scottish life in years to come, from North Sea oilfield transport to air-sea rescue, it is appropriate that Weir's had so much to do with developing the helicopter.

And there were other Scots. David Kay of Scone invented his own rotorcraft, known as the Kay Gyroplanes, the first version of which was built by Shields Garage in Perth. The well-known Scots engineers and instruments-makers, Barr and Stroud, also had a part to play in Kay's creation.

With the Second World War, the Weir aviation department was diverted to more pressing work - and Britain agreed that America should continue the development of helicopters. This was to prove disastrous for the helicopter ambitions of the Scots in the post-war world.

The work of Sikorsky and others put the Americans well ahead. Courageously, the Glasgow firm resumed its efforts, believing it had ideas to outdo Sikorsky, in matters like crop-spraying and heavier payloads.

Cierva's built the largest helicopter of its day, the Air Horse, powered by a Rolls-Royce Merlin engine, which passed muster at the Farnborough Air Show of 1949. In June 1950 Air Horse took off with a crew of three but metal fatigue caused a small component to fail - and the helicopter crashed, killing all three men.

The Ministry of Supply withdrew its interest and the Cierva company was heading for insolvency. Saunders-Roe took over all that was left of the Cierva business.

The final irony was that, before the collapse, the company had been developing a light machine known as the Skeeter. It was that machine which was the ancestor of the successful military helicopters we later came to know.

The Scots have a well-deserved reputation as engineers and inventors. What a pity that so much of the nation's genius seems to end up in other people's hands.

One man who has kept the success of the autogyro in his own hands is Jim Montgomerie from Crosshill, Maybole in Ayrshire, whose agricultural engineering business found itself under the influence of the boss's enthusiasm for aviation.

In 1986 Montgomerie Engineering was turning out its own autogyro and began collecting awards for its design and ingenuity. It set up records for flights between Scotland, the Isle of Man and Ireland and gained the world record for the longest sea crossing by this class of aircraft.

The autogyro may be a fun machine but it has become good business for one corner of Ayrshire.

This Bolkow 105 is operated by Strathclyde Police and is seen here at the City Centre Heliport alongside the River Clyde

Montgomerie built Autogyro G–BUJK at Kilkerran Airstrip in the 1990s. By 1994, the company had built 47 aircraft

Montgomerie Gyro–2 two-seat trainer with some of the team – Colin Aitken, Douglas Boyd, Jim Montgomerie, Heather Shearlaw & Craig Jones

From the invention of the aeroplane to the building of reliable models was one substantial step. But another massive leap was needed to harness this new and dramatic form of transport and to find its proper niche alongside the existing network of roads, railways and shipping.

Inevitably, it would call for the ingenuity of adventurous business minds (we now call them entrepreneurs) and it would almost certainly develop into something of a jungle before it was sorted out. As always, however, there were men for the moment, stamping upon different areas of Scotland their distinctive surnames, like Fresson in the north, Gandar Dower in the north-east and Sword in the west.

As an initiation of air transport, there were novel happenings in 1919 when, first Sholto Douglas (later Marshal of the Royal Air Force and Chairman of British European Airways) speeded up newspaper delivery by piloting a Handley Page over Dundee, Montrose and Aberdeen to drop bundles by parachute. In the same year, the emergency of a railway strike was overcome when a de Havilland was used to carry the mail between London and Glasgow. Soon afterwards, they were using a plane to deliver the first grouse from the Scottish moors to a London hotel.

To a generation still getting used to the novelty of the motor car, the aeroplane was just the latest excitement in a world gone mad about speed. Sir Alan Cobham had caused a stir by landing a flying boat at Leith and on the Clyde. Then in 1928 came a much-publicised race from London to Edinburgh between the railway's Flying Scotsman and an Armstrong Whitworth Argosy called the *City of Glasgow*. A three-engine biplane piloted by Captain G P Olley and carrying eighteen people, it made two stops for fuel on the flight from Croydon to Turnhouse and beat the train by a mere fifteen minutes.

One aviation enthusiast who had been flying in China, Captain Edmund Ernest Fresson, came north from Cheshire to give joyrides and one-man air displays in Scotland, drawing crowds all the way from Dumfries and Stranraer to Turriff, Huntly and Elgin, from Kirriemuir to Kirkwall.

All the time he was surveying the possibilities of air routes and by 1933 had chosen Inverness as his base, becoming managing director of Highland Airways, with a starting route from Inverness to Wick and Kirkwall. Captain Fresson's chairman was the boss of Macrae and Dick, well-known Inverness bus operators, an early sign of the interest being shown by the leaders of other forms of transport.

In Edinburgh, the large bus company of Scottish Motor Traction (SMT) had already gained licences to fly between Newcastle and the north of Scotland. In the west of Scotland, a director of the SMT company, John C. Sword from Ayr, was starting up Midland and Scottish Air Ferries which, by 1933, had a route from Renfrew to Campbeltown and on to Belfast, enabling passengers to spend several hours in Northern Ireland before returning to Glasgow by teatime.

As routes to the islands developed, Sword's company included one of the first women commercial pilots and engineers, the youthful Winifred Joyce Drinkwater. His planes ranged from Dragon Moths to the Avro Ten.

John Sword was shaping towards considerable success with this new-fangled form of transport, ordering an Avro 642 Sixteen, a high-wing monoplane carrying two pilots and sixteen passengers. It arrived in time for the inauguration of the Midland and Scottish service which would join up London, Glasgow and Belfast for the first time. The Prime Minister, Scotland's Ramsay MacDonald, was there to christen the new plane.

But Sword's success in the air was causing concern to powerful railway interests which had found a place on the SMT board. Bluntly, he was told to choose between his bus and aviation commitments and he decided on the former.

His Midland and Scottish Air Ferries therefore stopped flying in 1934, sadly bringing to an end the pioneering work of a far-seeing and

Winifred Drinkwater as a young pilot and engineer about to swing the prop to start a Dragon Moth

distinguished Scot. John Sword deserves a very high place in Scotland's aviation history.

In July 1934 the North-east of Scotland came into the picture through another energetic pioneer, E L Gandar Dower, who opened up his airfield at the village of Dyce, outside Aberdeen, which remains the basis of the Aberdeen Airport we know today.

Gandar Dower was soon running a twice weekly service between Aberdeen and Glasgow, flying a Short Scion and a Dragon Moth, followed by a route from Aberdeen to Wick, Thurso and Orkney. Then he established an Aberdeen-to-Edinburgh route to give Aberdonians a link to London.

In 1937 the name was changed to Allied Airways (Gandar Dower) Ltd and in that year the enterprising founder was even running a five-times-a-week service from Newcastle to Stavanger in Norway, little knowing the significant ties which that town would form with Aberdeen a generation later, through North Sea oil.

But where did those pioneers come from? Gandar Dower is a name worth examination. From a background in London and Brighton, he graduated in law at Cambridge and became a naval pilot in the First World War. But he had also become a poet and something of a Shakespearean actor so it was not surprising that he turned to the new romance of flying for a career.

Having established a base in Aberdeen in the early 1930s, he then flew with the RAF during the Second World War. When his airline was taken over by British European Airways after the war, he became Conservative MP for Caithness and Sutherland from 1945-50. Although he went to live in Guernsey, he returned to Aberdeen to be married, for the first time, at the age of 83 - and died in 1987, when he was 92.

If the bus companies were interested in flying, the railways were not be be left out. The four main companies, the LMS, the LNER, the Great Western and the Southern, came together with Imperial Airways to form Railway Air Services, an operation which included flying the Royal Mail between Glasgow, Belfast, Manchester, Birmingham and London.

Northern and Scottish Airways added another dimension to commercial flying, with flights to the islands which included an ambulance service. Campbeltown, Benbecula and Skye were among the destinations and, in 1936, the Air Ministry issued a licence to allow flying from the foreshore at the North Bay of Barra.

Air transport, which was mushrooming to the point of confusion, was brought to a sudden halt with the outbreak of the Second World War in September 1939. But it soon resumed, under Government control, with the aircraft now sporting a uniform camouflage of dark brown and green. Functions could vary, even to the point of helping with the evacuation of France in 1940.

There was even a new service to Stavanger in Norway from Perth and Dyce, for which British Airways (yes, that name had existed before) used the German-built Junkers aircraft. That was interrupted by the German invasion of Norway and Denmark in 1940 but, with Sweden's neutrality, a Swedish airline was able to maintain a service from Stockholm to Dyce, during which one of the planes was attacked by German fighters.

With the offices of the German airline Lufthansa situated close to the Swedish office of the British Overseas Airways Corporation, it was later discovered that, for five years, details of British air movement were being transmitted to the Luftwaffe in Norway.

From 1940 onwards Prestwick came into its own as the reception point for American-built military aircraft coming to sustain the war effort in Europe. Thousands of aircraft crossed what came to be known as the Atlantic Bridge, with BOAC operating the North Atlantic Return Ferry Service, ensuring that there was a steady flow of pilots being returned to Canada to keep the planes coming.

In view of the gauntness which settled on Prestwick at a later stage in the century, it is worth recording that, with all that wartime activity, it was then the busiest international airport in the world.

After the war, it took time to sort out air patterns. British European Airways (BEA) became a corporation in its own right, as distinct from BOAC, and by 1950 was operating a Glasgow-Manchester-Paris service. Then a Vickers Viscount became the first turbine-engined aircraft on domestic passenger flights, running between Edinburgh and London.

In 1951 the modified Dakota was recognised as the new Pionair class which could be found hopping its way from Glasgow, Edinburgh and Aberdeen to London.

So the post-war revolution continued into the 1960s with the appearance at Prestwick of giants like the Boeing 707 jetliners and the arrival of the Vanguard on the Glasgow-London route.

But the biggest event of the 1960s in Scotland was the final closing of Renfrew Airport in 1966 and the move two miles along the road to the former military airfield of Abbotsinch, which became the brand-new Glasgow Airport. All the pioneering and experimental work of the 1930s had come to fruition with an air transport system which was now established and flourishing.

Inaugural flight from Renfrew to Campbeltown in April 1933 by Midland & Scottish Air Ferries Fox Moth with "Daily Express" newspapers

SMT DH Fox Moth G–ACEB
at Corstorphine, Edinburgh
c.1933

Fresson's Highland Airways
Monospar G–ACEW at Longman
Airfield, Inverness in the mid '30s

DH 84 Dragon G–ACDL of
Midland & Scottish pleasure
flying from the beach at
Prestwick in 1933

First air mail to North
Ronaldsay in Scottish Airways
DH 84 Dragon G–ACIT,
31 July 1939

DH 84 Dragon G–ADFI "Silver
Ghost" and Short Scion G–ACUV
of Gandar Dower at Stromness
in the mid '30s

Gandar Dower's DH 86B
G–AETM "The Norseman" on
the Newcastle – Stavanger
service in the late 1930s

Loading the Shetland mails at
Thurso in January 1937 in the
first Air Mail service to the Islands

Autumn 1934 at Renfrew – on the ground are a Fox Moth of SMT, DH 86s of Railway Air Services and Imperial Airways, a Dragon of Midland & Scottish Air Ferries and a Scion of Aberdeen Airways whose Dragon (ex-Hillman Airways) is in the hangar. In the air are a Monospar of Highland Airways, an Airspeed Ferry of Midland & Scottish and two DH Moths

27

John Rae (chief pilot) and Jimmy Orrell of Midland & Scottish Air Ferries show off their new uniforms said to be modelled on that of a chauffeur!

Captain E E Fresson and Captain"Tug" Wilson with their Highland Airways DH 84 Dragon G–ADCT "Orcadian" at Longman in January 1938

*DH 89 Dragon Rapide G–ADDE "The Aberdonian" and DH 84 Dragon G–ACAN "The Starling"
of Aberdeen Airways over The Old Man of Hoy in 1936*

Ted Fresson, in leather flying coat, and passengers having just arrived at Inverness after a flight from Kirkwall in the Monospar G–ACEW

Midland & Scottish Avro 10 at Renfrew with Mary Drinkwater (Co. secy), John Sword (in bowler hat), A F Drinkwater (Winnie's father, no hat) and others

Spartan Cruiser G–ACYK of Scottish Airways over Glasgow University in the 1930s

Scottish Airways in wartime – DH 89A Dragon Rapide G–AGIC at Inverness (Longman) in 1945

FLIGHTS OF MERCY

A light aeroplane battling its way through an Atlantic storm on a flight of mercy, seeking out a windswept beach or rugged airstrip, is the stuff of television drama. It has also been the reality for many a pilot and accompanying nurse as they risked their lives to snatch the sick from a remote Scottish island and take them to the emergency ward of a city hospital.

Since the 1930s, the Scottish Air Ambulance Service has performed its daily task with a warm sense of vocation and a cool acceptance of unspoken danger, to the point where it now embarks on upwards of a thousand mercy missions every year.

Four fixed-wing planes and four helicopters stand poised at strategic points around Scotland, awaiting that call from the control centre in Aberdeen and ready for that flight which could mean the difference between life and death on some helpless island.

It is a service which has fashioned its own folk heroes, pilots like David Barclay and Eric Starling and nurses like Gisela Thurauf, and earned the gratitude of a remote population which had to learn before most to put their trust in those new-fangled contraptions.

The service came into operation in May 1933, based at Renfrew, when Midland and Scottish Air Ferries took delivery of two twin-engined Dragon Moths, fitted out as flying ambulances. On the very next day the first call came from Dr Stewart of Bruichladdich on the island of Islay, by way of a telegram: PLEASE SEND AIRPLANE IMMEDIATELY TO ISLAY. URGENT CASE. A 33-year-old fisherman, John McDermid, was suffering from perforation of the stomach and peritonitis was an immediate danger.

Captain Jimmy Orrell took off as the first in an illustrious line of mercy pilots. Forty-five minutes later he landed on the sands near Bridgend and picked up his patient, along with Mrs A W Ferguson, a nurse from Glasgow who happened to be on holiday there.

An ambulance was waiting at Renfrew to rush Mr McDermid to the Western Infirmary, Glasgow, where he underwent the emergency operation. He was discharged 25 days later, completely recovered. Aviation had found a new role on that historic night – and the basic pattern remains to this day.

Naturally that first mission was a major news item, headlined in the Scottish Daily Express as: DEATH DEFEATED BY SCOTS PLANE DASH. Thereafter it simply developed in more routine fashion. The first flight to Skye, two months later, uplifted a Dr Fothergill, who took ill while on holiday at Uig, and flew him through a dramatic thunderstorm to Edinburgh Royal Infirmary.

Four years later, Shetland joined the Bed-in-the-Clouds Club when lighthouse keeper Alex MacRae took seriously ill. Captain Vallance peered through a lifting fog and managed to identify the strip of grass which had been cleared by Mr MacRae's son and daughter, bringing his Dragon Moth to within 50 yards of the lighthouse.

So the dramas built up over the years, so often linked to the personal stories of the air crews involved. David Barclay, a dairyman's son from Greenock, became idolised as the pilot who would fly, they said, even when the birds were walking.

He had joined the RAF in 1929 and went to India, flying in the mysterious beauty of the North West Frontier. But Barclay felt the tug of more worthwhile service back home and, by the mid-1930s, was back in Scotland, flying his air ambulance out of Renfrew, becoming the personal friend of the island population and giving most of his career to their welfare.

There were occasions when he would battle through a snowstorm to pick up a child whose life depended on his arrival – a child whose parents he would

The first air ambulance flight. On 14 May 1933 DH 84 Dragon, G-ACCZ of Midland & Scottish Air Ferries piloted by Jimmy Orrell, is seen with patient at Renfrew

know well. After one frightening experience in a Rapide which iced up and took him just narrowly over a mountain top, he advocated a more sophisticated aircraft and that was how the Heron came to service.

David Barclay gained the MBE and also became the only British airline pilot to receive the Order of St John of Jerusalem. When he retired in 1965, at the age of 60, his last visit to the islands turned into a moving public tribute. The folk came out en masse and, as he prepared to leave the beach at Barra, he mounted the steps of his aircraft, turned and raised his arm in salute.

Dipping one last time to the waving crowd he headed back to Renfrew, to be met by scores of well-wishers, with Flight Manager Eric Starling leading a special guard of honour. Such was the rapport of that remarkable service. David Barclay died in 1981 at the age of 75.

As a colourful character of the skies few could equal the same Eric Starling, who was also closely associated with the ambulance service. Starling was born in St John's Wood, London, in 1911, son of a well-to-do jeweller, and by the age of 22 had notched up his own piece of aviation history, albeit of a rather infamous nature.

Sitting his commercial pilot's test in 1933, he was required to fly the 55 miles

Capt Eric Starling, BEA's Flight Manager in Scotland from 1949 to 1968, thereafter i/c Scottish Air Ambulance Service until his retiral in 1971, seen with a Heron on the beach at Barra

from Croydon to Lymnpe on a moonless night. Somehow he lost his bearings and, in a developing crisis, spotted a town of mysterious identity. He decided his best hope was to land on one of its well-lit streets - and that is what he did, colliding with a lamp-post. A jabbering, excited crowd gathered round to confirm the fact that he had come to rest in Calais!

The extraordinary happening reached the headlines and was read by another Englishman, the great E L Gandar Dower, who was planning to create an airport in Scotland. But first he had occasion to visit Gatwick, which was then a small private aerodrome, and there he was greeted by a tall young man.

"What's your name?" asked Gandar Dower.

"Starling," came the reply.

"Not that bloody fool who landed on a Calais street last week?"

"Yes."

"You're as mad as I am. I'm going to build an airport and start airlines at Aberdeen. Are you willing to join me?"

That was how Eric Starling landed in Scotland, one of several adventurous pilots who came north to pioneer air routes. From 1934 until 1971 he made history on many of those routes, striking out for Shetland (to an airfield not yet opened!) and across the North Sea. For him the Second World War began in the North Atlantic and ended with landing the first Allied aircraft in Rangoon after the Japanese withdrawal.

The post-war years were spent with British European Airways and his 40 years of flying ended at Abbostinch Airport, Glasgow, where he had become BEA's most senior and respected airline captain. In all that time, no passenger had received as much as a scratch in an aircraft under Starling's command.

From 1934 he was flying patients but not in the organised way of the service at Renfrew. The first case recorded in his log-book took place in February 1936 from St Margaret's Hope in Orkney. He remembers carrying, from Stromness to Aberdeen, a man whose false teeth were stuck in his throat! He flew his last ambulance run in December 1971. Into his eighties, Eric Starling was still living in West Kilbride, Ayrshire, one of the larger-than-life legends of flying.

When the air ambulance service was run from Glasgow, the nurses were supplied by the Southern General Hospital – a collection of brave women, typified by Gisela Thurauf, whose Bavarian family were refugees from Hitler.

Gisela flew on her first mission in 1965, received her "wings" in the customary way after ten flights – and flew with her 1000th patient from Benbecula to Glasgow in 1986. She was awarded the "Queen's Commendation for Valuable Service in the Air," the only woman to have received the award in that category.

Psychiatric patients could cause their own problems and Miss Thurauf was the one who encountered the man insisting that he should leave the plane in mid-flight – to attend mass! The nurse had to persuade him that it was too early for mass. And in any case, the altar boys had not yet arrived.

The original structure of the Scottish Air Ambulance Service changed somewhat in 1947, with the formation of the National Health Service and the creation of British European Airways, taking in the various independent Scottish airlines.

The two nationalised organisations worked together for the next 26 years till 1973, when the full air ambulance contract was taken over by Loganair. That lasted for the next 20 years, until there was a review of the service and further changes were made.

From 1993 the calls went through an Air Desk at Aberdeen and the service was provided jointly by Loganair's fixed-wing planes and Bond Helicopters. The various machines are stationed all the way from Lerwick and Kirkwall to Plockton, Aberdeen, Glasgow and Prestwick.

Scotland therefore has the first fully integrated air ambulance service in the United Kingdom. But the spirit stretches back to the days of those pioneers in the early thirties.

Kitty McPherson, who retired in 1980 as Loganair's manager at Barra, served with four airlines during her 44 year career. She is seen here with radio in hand guiding in a BEA Heron to the ambulance waiting on the beach

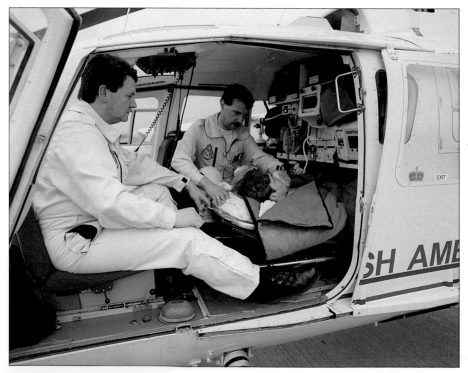

Crew and patient aboard one of the Bolkow 105 helicopters operated by Bond for the Scottish Ambulance Service

A Bolkow 105 and an Islander in the Air Ambulance yellow livery

FIRST FLIGHT OVER EVEREST

Though it has had to fight for survival in the latter part of the century, Prestwick International Airport was once the finest in Britain – and owes its existence above all to one remarkable man.

David Fowler McIntyre was a local boy of high ambition but the reality of his local airport might never have happened if he had not previously been chosen as one of two pilots who set out to "conquer" Mount Everest by flying over its summit.

The youngest of seven children, David was born in 1905, son of John McIntyre, managing director of the Ailsa Shipbuilding Company in Troon. His schools included Ayr Academy and Glasgow Academy but he had the one abiding passion which was aviation.

He took his first lesson at Beardmore's Flying School at Renfrew and in 1927 was commissioned in the Auxiliary Air Force (the "Territorials" of the air) as a Pilot Officer in No. 602 (City of Glasgow) Squadron.

David McIntyre was growing into a young man of striking appearance and boundless enthusiasm, the sort of chap known to smoke a cigarette to pass the time during a 10,000ft parachute jump!

But his big moment came in 1933 with the attempt on Everest, an idea put up by Colonel Stewart Blacker, grandson of the first Surveyor-General of India, and supported by John Buchan, the famous Scottish writer.

Looking for a senior pilot, Buchan asked his fellow-Member of Parliament, the Marquis of Clydesdale (the future Duke of Hamilton), who was then Squadron Leader of 602. Clydesdale took up the challenge and nominated David McIntyre as the other pilot.

Their expedition would seek to map and photograph unknown slopes, create a new altitude record for two-man flying, make a motion picture – and be tackled as a boost for Britain and her aviation industry.

The patriotic element stirred the financial support of Lady Lucy Houston and the party left for India with their two specially-converted Westland single-engined biplanes, a PV3 and a Wallace.

Stewart Blacker was flying as Clydesdale's observer and McIntyre had with him a Gaumont British cameraman who would make the film Wings Over Everest. McIntyre made the wind calculations which were vital to their success and reckoned, on the chosen April day, that they could stay around the mountain top for only about 15 minutes.

They soared into a world of new vistas and were only minutes from the top when they were blown off course by mounting winds. Nothing was predictable. Pounding for the summit, McIntyre was suddenly hauled back 2000ft by a downrush of air. He took the buffeting, kept his head and was lucky to be lifted by an up-current which took him scraping over the summit of Everest.

The two pilots had lost sight of each other and McIntyre didn't know that Clydesdale was already over the peak. Meanwhile the cameraman knocked himself unconscious by tramping on his oxygen pipe.

But Everest had been conquered in the aerial sense, an achievement just within the capabilities of the time, and now it was back to earth, but only to discover that the survey cameras had not functioned properly, to the detriment of the map-making programme.

Clydesdale and McIntyre wanted to retrieve the situation but the powers back in London, not least the insurers, ordered no more risks. The two heroes, however, feigned a touch of ignorance and quietly took off again.

Conquering Everest for the second time, they succeeded with the survey cameras and were duly forgiven their disobedience.

In fact the whole world knew about their achievement and two Scots came home to a joyous welcome, before being awarded the Air Force Cross.

Clydesdale and McIntyre had written themselves into the history books – and were back with fresh inspiration for what might be next on their horizons.

The Marquis of Clydesdale

Sqn Ldr D F McIntyre DFC

The Westland PV3 (modified Wallace) being flown by The Marquis of Clydesdale over Mount Everest

MOLLISON AND McKELLAR

The spirit of aviation which stirred with the rise of the century was personified, in their own contrasting ways, by two remarkable Scottish pilots.

Among their many common factors, Jim Mollison and Archie McKellar were both Glasgow lads who, like many of their generation, had been inspired by boyhood tales of the early flying legends.

Mollison, born in Pollokshields in 1905, grew up to be himself one of the great pioneers of the air while McKellar, Paisley-born in 1912 before the family moved to Glasgow, emerged as a legend of the Battle of Britain, personally accounting for upwards of 16 German planes in that crucial and historic episode of the Second World War.

Curiously, while the whole world came to idolise Amy Johnson, the fish merchant's daughter from Hull who was the first woman to fly solo from England to Australia, there were many Scots who didn't seem to realise that her husband, Jim Mollison, whose feats in the air were equal to hers, was one of themselves. Perhaps his flamboyance looked out of character in a race which can sometimes boast about its modesty!

Jim Mollison was indeed a swashbuckling character in that pre war mould of Hollywood glamour, he and Amy taking their place as international celebrities, rubbing shoulders with the Clark Gables, the Robert Montgomerys and the Douglas Fairbankses.

Jim Mollison

In fact Douglas Fairbanks Jnr was sent by Warner Brothers in an attempt to interest the Scot in a flying film, not only as technical adviser but, with his good looks and charm, as an actor alongside Fairbanks and the up-and-coming Bette Davis.

Jim Mollison didn't take up the film star role but he certainly became known as a hard-drinking womaniser of the type who could have delivered, with a natural ease, the Rhett Butler line of: "Frankly my dear, I don't give a damn!"

Mollison was born in the red-sandstone tenement at 33 Fotheringay Road Glasgow, grandson of the substantial James Mollison, Lloyd's surveyor in Scotland who became a town councillor for Partick.

Jim's father, Hector, described as "a rotter and a drunkard," was paid off to disappear to Australia and the boy was brought up by his mother, Thomasina Addie, who came from a well-to-do shipping family.

They moved to addresses like 21 York Drive, Hyndland, and 42 Falkland Mansions, and Jim attended Glasgow Academy. At 18 he joined the RAF and set out for Duxford, waved off at Glasgow Central by his mother.

It was the start of a highly colourful career, the learning process for all those skills which would turn him into such a legend of the 1930s, perhaps the greatest of all the long-distance solo pilots feted during that period with the same kind of hero-worship as the astronauts of a generation later.

America had produced Charles Lindbergh, in 1927 the first man to fly eastward across the Atlantic, and Amelia Earhart, who became the first woman to do so a year later. England's Amy Johnson kept up the British end with her solo flight to Australia in 1930.

But it was left to Scotland's Jim Mollison to do what Lindbergh knew to be

Amy Johnson, Winnie Drinkwater, Jim Mollison at Renfrew, early 1930s

the difficult one, of flying westward across the Atlantic. He achieved that in 1932, the same year in which he made the first trans-Sahara flight to South Africa – and married Amy Johnson. They were the couple in the news. If they appeared in

A Mardi Gras reception for Mollison and his wife Amy Johnson in New York on 1 August 1933 after their first direct flight from UK to USA. The flight took 39 hours in a DH 84 Dragon, G-ACCV "Seafarer". Mollison likened this reception to "a Caesar bringing home to Rome a new Empress". 200,000 cheering New Yorkers unleashed a summer snowstorm of welcome to the first man and wife team to fly to their country from Europe.

the royal box at the London Palladium the audience would rise in thunderous applause.

In 1933 they flew together in the first direct flight from the United Kingdom to the United States, after which they were given the freedom of New York, with its ticker-tape welcome.

Mollison also made the first non-stop westward flight across the South Atlantic and gained the admiration of Charles Lindbergh. The American was anxious to meet this Scottish hero despite the fact that he was keeping a low profile after the kidnap and murder of his baby son, the scandal which had recently shocked the world. So the two men met very privately in New York.

Mollison's proud grandfather, the Glasgow ex-Baillie, was still alive to savour the triumphs and to see his native city honour him at a civic reception.

The glamour of the great aviators was, however, beginning to wear off and the gathering clouds of war symbolised trouble in the Mollison marriage as well. Jim and Amy were finally divorced in 1938 but he was to go through two more divorces and a string of affairs which rather tarnished his reputation.

In the Second World War both he and Amy Johnson flew as ferry pilots in the Air Transport Auxiliary. In January 1941 she had delivered an Airspeed Oxford to Prestwick and was taking another one back south to Kidlington when she suspected the compass was reading incorrectly.

At that moment Jim was delivering another aircraft in the south of England, little knowing that his ex-wife was running into bad weather, low cloud and serious trouble over the Thames Estuary.

Mystery surrounded her eventual fate. From one sailor in the vicinity there was the report of a woman's voice in the water calling "Hurry, please hurry!" The nation would not have appreciated the news that its own heroine had been mistakenly shot down by our own ships and coastal defences. But that seems the likely answer.

There had been a hint of Amy and Jim getting together again, a romantic conclusion which would have delighted the public (if not his latest wife!) so it was hardly surprising that he was devastated by her death and went more and more into his shell, seeking more and more comfort from the bottle.

Despite the playboy lifestyle, Mollison maintained a serious interest in aviation and had a meeting with scientists to discuss the possibility of space travel, offering himself for any venture to the Moon.

He went to be dried out after losing his flying licence for heavy drinking in 1953. By the time he was into his fifties he was scarcely able to walk and he finally died in 1959, aged 54, from a severe form of alcoholism. His mother survived to attend the memorial service at Christ Church, Mayfair.

Jim Mollison, whose Glasgow birthplace at 33 Fotheringay Road bears a plaque in his memory, had helped to blaze the trail for air routes across the world, showing what would be possible with more sophisticated equipment when so much could be done by one man in a light plane which had neither radio nor any other fancy gadget.

He focused attention on air travel and fired the imagination of youngsters like Archie McKellar, who was born at 4 Southpark Drive, Paisley, before the family moved into Glasgow, where his father had a plasterer's business.

At five-feet-three, Archie was remembered as "a great wee scrapper" at Shawlands Academy, developing into a determined little hard man at rugby but a beautifully smooth mover in the ballroom.

He wanted to be a plasterer like his father, who managed instead to persuade him into a stockbroker's office, Miller and Cooper at 48 West George Street, Glasgow. But he had his way in the end and served a full apprenticeship with his father. The main ambition, however, was to be a pilot and for once he defied his father, who dwelt on the dangers, and took secret lessons with Glasgow Flying Club at Renfrew. Gaining his pilot's licence, he flew low over his home in Bearsden, waggled the wings of his Tiger Moth – and dropped a box of chocolates for his mother's birthday! It was apparently typical of wee Archie.

It was also the start of a career in which he would become known as one of the bravest and most skilful pilots ever to grace the skies. He was soon noticed by the Marquis of Clydesdale, himself one of the heroes for his flight over Everest, who invited him to join 602 City of Glasgow Squadron.

Gaining his RAF wings in 1937, he was now part of that invaluable reserve of weekend flyers who would soon come to save the nation's bacon. By the Second World War they were equipped with Spitfires and Archie's early involvement with German planes is told in the chapter about action over the Forth in the late autumn of 1939.

During an eight-month lull in activity, which Archie found irksome, the Glasgow squadron found itself joined at Drem, East Lothian, by No. 605 Squadron, just back from action at Dunkirk.

He struck up a friendship with 605's commander, Walter Churchill, who was so impressed that he invited him to take up a vacancy in his squadron. So Archie joined his new colleagues, now flying a Hurricane instead of a Spitfire, and was soon in action over Newcastle, when they waded into a swarm of German planes and shot down eight of them, Archie himself accounting for at least three. Flight Lieutenant McKellar was awarded the Distinguished Flying Cross.

Now it was south to Croydon and the Battle of Britain, counteracting the Luftwaffe planes which were coming in by the hundred, wave after wave. Archie McKellar was in his element, darting, harrying, chasing and destroying these enemy raiders. During one attack over Maidstone his Squadron Leader, Walter Churchill, saw him swinging in to attack three Heinkels from behind. Suddenly they turned and came straight for Archie in tight formation.

He blasted the leading Heinkel, which blew up and knocked the wing off one of its neighbours. Then he dealt with the other one and all three went plunging

Sandy Johnstone and Archie McKellar of 602 Squadron at Drem in March 1940

to the ground, destroyed in a matter of seconds by one wee man from Glasgow.

On 15 September 1940, officially named as Battle of Britain Day, Archie bagged another three Germans by himself and his exploits in that decisive battle were already becoming well known.

Succeeding Walter Churchill as commander of 605, he and his squadron were diverted to Westhampnett, where he found himself in brief re-union with his former colleagues of 602 from Glasgow, including old friends like Sandy Johnstone.

By then, however, the pressure was beginning to show and Sandy thought Archie looked tired and weary. Yet he had just returned from shooting down five more Messerschmitts and was refusing to take leave while the battle raged.

As commander, he now had the added burden of writing harrowing letters to bereaved parents. When one of his sergeant pilots was reported missing over Romney Marsh, the father and brother set out to search – and found the lad's body still strapped in his cockpit. All the tragedies had to be absorbed in Britain's fight for survival.

In his few weeks at Croydon Archie had shot down 17 enemy planes and damaged many more, putting him near the top of the list of those pilots whom Churchill chose to call "The Few."

Despite all the strains, the bouncy, jovial Glaswegian, who kept them all going with his native wit and humour, seemed to lead that charmed life which can favour the super-optimist.

One of his colleagues, Chris Currant, came back from a short rest and was shaving when Archie came in. "Why are you up at this time?" he asked. Chris said he was getting ready for operations. "There's no need to, old lad" said Archie. "I'm doing your turn this morning so that you can rest till afternoon."

It was 7.50am on 1 November 1940 when Archie took to the air, engaging in a dogfight on the Kent side of the Thames Estuary. But he became separated from his friends and would seem to have gone "hunting" on his own. He paid a dear price.

His Hurricane was seen plunging crazily to the ground from a great height. A German plane believed to be his last victim was lying nearby. One of the RAF's greatest-ever pilots was gone. Said Chris Currant, the man whose place he took that morning: "For days I just couldn't accept that he was dead. It seemed impossible."

But the wee man was at peace, right enough, brought back for burial in his beloved Glasgow. The Marquis of Clydesdale and Lord Provost Patrick Dollan were among those present.

Archie knew everybody and the wreaths included one from girls in a flower shop and another from the car-park attendant at St Enoch's Station.

He already had a Bar to his DFC and now he had a DSO. His father went to Buckingham Palace to collect his honours from King George VI, remembering well how he had warned him of the dangers of flying but fiercely proud of him nevertheless.

The Battle of Britain ended officially at midnight on 31 October, eight hours before Archie McKellar was killed. Sadly, the man who was one of the inspirations of that great battle does not appear on its roll of honour. You would have thought they could have stretched the rule for a hero who was at the very heart of that victory.

Charcoal portrait of Archie McKellar when he was with 602 Squadron

THE PRESTWICK STORY

If future generations are appalled at the decline of Scotland's manufacturing industries in the late 20th century, they will at least be heartened by the story of aircraft design and production at Prestwick.

The fact that the Jetstream model managed to capture a world lead in the market for small turboprop regional aircraft has been an immense achievement, heightened in the 1990s by the development of the 64-seater Advanced TurboProp (ATP) into the Jetstream 61, the largest production plane ever built in Scotland.

This modern battle to keep Scotland in the forefront of a world market is undertaken in the name of Jetstream Holdings, the corporate identity of British Aerospace at Prestwick.

But the root of the whole enterprise was a company called Scottish Aviation - and that takes us back to those two local heroes of the 1930s, David McIntyre and the Marquis of Clydesdale, who came home from their aerial conquest of Mount Everest with a burning ambition to establish an aviation industry in their native land.

Both young men, the shipbuilder's son McIntyre and the aristocratic Clydesdale (later to be the Duke of Hamilton), had been commanding officers of the City of Glasgow Squadron. But the first step towards their ambition came when the growing threat of Nazi Germany forced Britain to expand the Royal Air Force with the consequent need to train more crews.

The Government was offering training contracts to private companies which would provide their own planes and airfields and give pilots their first 50 hours of instruction. Clydesdale's personal acquaintance with directors of the big De Havilland company brought enough backing to enable the two enthusiasts to set up Scottish Aviation in 1935.

McIntyre became a director but Clydesdale's brother had to take his place on the board since he himself was then a Member of Parliament.

McIntyre was among those who had observed that Prestwick had a freakish record of fog-free weather and was therefore an ideal spot for an airfield. So the new company bought a stretch of farmland on the Monkton side of the Pow Burn, near the Orangefield Hotel, and No. 12 Elementary & Reserve Flying Training School opened in 1936, amid local objections about noise and with an undertaking not to fly on Sundays until the kirk bells announced the end of the morning service!

The personal appeal of McIntyre and Clydesdale, not to mention their skill and ambition, soon brought high success to the training scheme at Prestwick. They needed 20 Tiger Moths to cope with initial demand and the first course was completed in little more than half the time expected.

David McIntyre took his share of tuition alongside flying instructors who were guaranteed an income of £500 a year, a respectable sum in the 1930s. Potential pilots needed Higher English and Maths and two Lowers and were paid a shilling an hour of attendance money plus their bus fares from Glasgow.

They later came to train observers, navigators and wireless operators and in the five years to 1941 Prestwick turned out 1,334 pilots and nearly 2,000 observers, more than half the total in the RAF at that time. Scottish Aviation had topped the table by turning out five times as many air crews as any other centre in Britain.

With the Second World War under way, the early phase of Scottish Aviation's history was coming to an end, following a decision to move training courses to countries like Canada and South Africa.

Prestwick had become an RAF station, with David McIntyre as the Group Captain in command, but he and his company had also turned their attention from the training of aircrew to the possibility of building the planes themselves.

The Scottish Aviation factory had started in a small way before the war and was now expanding dramatically. The huge Palace of Engineering, which had been a feature of the great Empire Exhibition at Bellahouston Park, Glasgow, in 1938, was dismantled and re-erected at Prestwick.

Then came a curious stroke of fate. One of the first aircraft to be sent to Britain from North America during the war lost its way in bad weather and landed at Prestwick instead of the intended Aldergrove in Northern Ireland. Few at Prestwick paid much attention but, out of the misadventure, the Scottish airfield was named as the terminus for this new air bridge which would be so active in the succeeding years

McIntyre was not slow to grasp the opportunity and his company was soon repairing and modifying a wide range of aeroplanes, gaining experience of American ones.

Even in the midst of the war he was also publishing plans of his dream for a post-war Prestwick, asking Government recognition for an international airport. Having become a throbbing centre of wartime activity, it was widely acknowledged as the finest airport in Britain by 1945. It is interesting to consider that, at that point, Heathrow and Northolt, serving London, were the poor relations with nothing more than a field and a few huts.

Extending his vision in all directions, McIntyre planned his Scottish Airlines to take advantage of what would surely be the popular mode of travel after the war . That ambition would come unstuck with nationalisation of the airline industry, as part of the post-war Labour Government's comprehensive plan for public ownership.

Scottish Aviation also fought against compulsory purchase of its Prestwick property but that too went into public ownership and they became tenants of what they once possessed.

Prestwick did get its new terminal in 1964, opened by the Queen Mother, but by then a political battle had been engaged for the development of Abbotsinch as the new Glasgow Airport. Despite a courageous stand, Prestwick has tended to be on the losing end of that battle ever since, with Glasgow capturing the international routes as well as the domestic.

That left aircraft manufacture and McIntyre and his company were the only Scottish enterprise involved in that after the war. His ambition now was to produce a plane designed and built entirely in Scotland. The chance came with a services requirement for a five-seater model capable of short take-off and landing.

That was how Scottish Aviation came to create the Prestwick Pioneer, first flown in 1947 and proving invaluable in the subsequent campaigns in the Malayan jungles.

It was followed by the Twin Pioneer, carrying 16 passengers, which first flew in 1955. Apart from his skill and ambition, David McIntyre was the kind of man who knew all his employees by name and there are wonderful stories of him arriving at the factory to join his night-shift workers at their break – complete with fish suppers and crates of beer to cater for everyone!

McIntyre was the kind of visionary whose battles for Scotland deserved a better fate. But the fates themselves were not on his side in 1957 when modifications were carried out on the twin Pioneers as the result of a crash. The only plane still to be modified was the one with which David McIntyre was due to undertake a sales drive in North Africa. It would take only a couple of days but he couldn't wait.

His first stop was Libya, where he was giving a demonstration flight. But the plane failed to return and the wreckage was found in the desert 300 miles from Tripoli. The port wing had fallen off and he and five others were killed.

Twin Pioneer production was continued, with Mr T D M Robertson as managing director, and in a period of diversification Scottish Aviation took on the overhaul of Rolls-Royce and Pratt Whitney engines.

In 1965, contracts were secured to build wings for the Handley Page Jetstream and sections of the Hercules for Lockheed-Georgia. In 1966 Scottish Aviation became part of the Cammell Laird Group and, when Handley Page and Beagle Aircraft failed, the Scots company beat keen competition to build large numbers of the Bulldog trainer aircraft.

In 1978 Scottish Aviation became a subsidiary of the state-owned British Aerospace and there were plans for a new Jetstream, that name which dated back to Handley Page days.

There were rumoured doubts about the future of the Prestwick factory, however, and talk of production being moved south. But the crisis passed and Jetstream 31, a 19-seater, went on to record a remarkable success.

By the mid–1980s they were looking at the next stage of the plane, the Jetstream 41, which stretched the fuselage of its predecessor by 14 feet and provided 29 seats.

The operations director, Mr Allan MacDonald, battled to improve efficiency, with the result that productivity rose to levels unequalled anywhere in British Aerospace. Instead of Prestwick, it was an English plant which closed and the Scots inherited production of the Advanced TurboProp (ATP) for which British Airways has been placing orders in the 1990s.

Indeed, MacDonald's positive talk and firm commitment to the future of Prestwick carried echoes of David McIntyre himself.

The remains of that extraordinary man, without whom there would probably have been no trace of an aviation story at Prestwick at all, lie buried in the kirkyard of Alloway, a few miles away in the heartland of Robert Burns.

But as long as his spirit survives, there will be hope for this shining example of Scottish enterprise at its hard-working best.

A Fokker F.22, an Anson and a Tiger Moth of No. 12 Elementary & Reserve Flying Training School and No. 1 Air Observers Navigation School seen in 1940

Dundonald, a satelite of Prestwick, was home to No. 516 Combined Operations Squadron RAF in 1944 whose Blenheim is seen here

This USAAF B-17 Flying Fortress landed at Dundonald in error mistaking it for Prestwick. It damaged the runway and had to be dismantled to get it out

Repair work in the "Palace" during the war reveals Spitfires, B-24 Liberators and a B-17 Flying Fortress

The Termimal area at the end of the war with a C-54, DC-3s and a Lodestar

An RAF Liberator of No. 86 Squadron emerging from the "Palace" in August 1945

*"Full house" on the North Dispersal in 1945. Too many to count but types include
B-24 Liberator, Lancaster, Wellington, B-17 Flying Fortress, C-54 Skymaster and C-47 Dakota*

Scottish Airlines first
DC-3 Dakota G–AGWS
at Prestwick in 1947

Scottish Airlines Liberator
Freighter G–AHDY at
Prestwick

Liberator SX–DAA
"Hellas" of the Scottish
Aviation operated
Hellenic Airlines in 1950

Prototype Prestwick
Pioneer, VL515, as built
with a Gypsy Queen
engine flying in 1947

Pioneer CC1, XE512,
demonstrating its short
take off capabilities at
Prestwick

Pioneer CC1, XE515,
flying for real with the
RAF in Malaya

Twin Pioneer produc-
tion in the old 'Fokker'
hangar (now used by
the BAe Flying College)

Robert McIntyre (no
relation to D F),
designer of the
Pioneer and Twin
Pioneer

Waco Hadrian, FR579 'Voo-Doo', was the first glider to be towed across the Atlantic landing at Prestwick on 1 July 1943. It is seen landing after its crossing as it passes two RAF Coastal Command B-17 Flying Fortresses

Trans World Airlines Boeing Stratoliner at Prestwick in 1942. It was one of the many aircraft which maintained the Atlantic Air Bridge during WWII

The USAF re-established its connection with Prestwick in November 1951 when the 1631st Air Base Group moved in. The 67th Air Rescue Squadron, whose SA-16B Albatross and SC-54D aircraft are seen here, remained untill 1966 although the USAF's Military Air Transport Service continued to use the airport until the closure of the submarine base in the Holy Loch

Canadian rescue facilities in the 1950s and early 60s were provided by Lancaster 10MRs like FM213 above from 107 Rescue Unit at Torbay. These aircraft continued in service until 1964.

RCAF Sabres at Prestwick prior to scrapping by Scottish Aviation in 1963. The 'Canadian connection' began in 1943 and continues with regular transport flights at the airport.

Scottish Aviation Bulldog T1s of the Universities of Glasgow & Strathclyde Air Squadron flying over Glasgow University

Jetstream 31, G–LOGR, on test at Prestwick before delivery to Loganair. These Jetstreams were the first Scottish built aircraft to be flown by a Scottish airline in scheduled service

Jetstream 31s for the Japanese J–AIR on test in Scotland in 1991

After the first flight of the J41 at Prestwick on 25 September 1991 managing director Allan MacDonald is seen with Ian Conradi (Chief Test Pilot), Pete Smith, John Whittaker, and Terry Mason (flight crew) and John Larroucau (Vice-President Engineering)

*Passengers boarding a Jetstream 41 , G–WAFT, of Manx Airlines
at Glasgow Airport in August 1994*

The first Jetstream 61, G–JXLI, over the Prestwick Plant in September 1994

*Engine maintenance for the world's airlines. A General electric CF6–6 engine being rebuilt
following overhaul at Aviall Caledonian Engine Services at Prestwick*

*Ryanair's daily services to Dublin, started in May 1994, are flown by
Boeing 737s and BAC 1-11s*

LORD DOWDING

Winston Churchill expressed the feelings of the nation when he said of those airmen who won the Battle of Britain in 1940: "Never in the field of human conflict was so much owed by so many to so few."

Less glory, however, was afforded the courageous Scot who masterminded that famous victory, Hugh Dowding from Moffat in Dumfriesshire, who was then in charge of Fighter Command. Dowding, a lonesome introvert, was said to have made an enemy of Churchill.

But he stuck to his guns, led us to victory, to find himself the only successful commander who was not made a Marshal of the Royal Air Force when it was all over. The controversial Dowding, who became a spiritualist, was allowed to retire amid much unease about the public neglect of such an able man. The subsequent feature film "Battle of Britain" was seen as a vindication of the great Scot.

Hugh Dowding's father was a master at Fettes School in Edinburgh but moved to the Borders to open a preparatory school in Moffat. It was there in 1882 that Hugh Dowding was born and there that he spent the first 15 years of his life. He joined the Royal Artillery in 1900 but switched to the Royal Flying Corps in 1914 and was decorated for his services in the First World War. By 1936 he was commander-in-chief of Fighter Command, the man who would be charged with the air defence of Britain in the war to come.

Whatever the national neglect of its famous son, Moffat made amends in 1972 by erecting a fine sandstone memorial in the town's park. Lord Dowding had died two years earlier but his widow was there on unveiling day. There was also an appeal that day to raise funds for the RAF Association Home at Sussexdown.

The appeal should have come in the address of another legend of the skies, Group Captain Douglas Bader, the legless pilot. On the way north, however, Bader was involved in a road accident, adding an extra touch of drama to the memorial day of a Scot whose life had not been short of it.

ROLLS-ROYCE

The name of Rolls-Royce is long established in the English language as a synonym for smooth perfection, whether in the motor cars which purr with aristocratic elegance or the great airliners which soar into the heavens with incomparable sophistication.

The story of how Charles Rolls and Henry Royce developed their partnership is one of the great tales of industrial history. How their enterprise found its way into Scotland, where it is still deeply involved in the creation of aero engines, is less well known.

But it is a part of aviation history which has touched the lives of thousands of Scots families since it all began at the outbreak of the Second World War. Up to 1939 the Rolls-Royce operation had been concentrated on Derby but the approach of war brought a need to disperse that production.

The Air Ministry had earmarked Hillington, on the outskirts of Glasgow, for one of its "shadow" factories, which meant it would be run on its behalf by Rolls-Royce.

The initial plan was to employ 15,000 people, aiming at a weekly production of 100 Merlin engines, the ones to power those Spitfires, Hurricanes and Lancasters which would play such a vital part in defeating the menace of Hitler.

In reality that workforce built up to a staggering 26,000 people, many of them women taking over from the men who were off to war.

The chief quality engineer throughout that war was an Edinburgh man, William Miller ('MR' as he was known within Rolls-Royce), who would play a crucial part in the whole future of Rolls-Royce in Scotland.

By the time that massive wartime organisation reached VE-Day in 1945, the workforce had been cut back to 15,000. The emergency of war was now over. Rolls-Royce would be returning to its peacetime activity in England and had no further interest in the tenancy of the Hillington and associated Scottish factories, which belonged to the Air Ministry.

By then William Miller had become general manager of Rolls-Royce in Scotland, in time to be given an order from headquarters in Derby: Close the Scottish plant and dismiss the remaining 15,000! His own future would be guaranteed with a plum job at Derby.

To his everlasting credit, Miller was not prepared to do it. At a time of mounting unemployment, he would fight to salvage Rolls-Royce in Scotland. The survival plan he devised was based on the fact that, with large numbers of British planes and Merlin engines now sold to foreign countries, there would be an on-going market for spares and repairs.

So he set off for Derby to see the managing director, Sir Arthur Sidgreaves,

'Hs with Mr'
Lord Hives, chairman of Rolls-Royce, and William Miller at Hillington in the 1950s

but was told: "You are wasting your time and, what's more, you're wasting mine. Go back to Scotland and get on with the job you've been given to do!"

Miller was putting his head on the chopping-block but he didn't flinch. Daringly, he by-passed Rolls-Royce and went to the Air Ministry to see P A Cook, a man he had known through the wartime connection.

If Cook could investigate and confirm this theory about a likely market, then give the contract to Rolls-Royce, he might suggest that the work should be done in Glasgow! Cook agreed to inquire, found that Miller was absolutely right – and went to see Rolls-Royce. By a stroke of luck for Scotland, the hostile Sir Arthur was about to retire and the proposition was judged instead by the new man, E W Hives, who persuaded the main board to accept it. This would save two

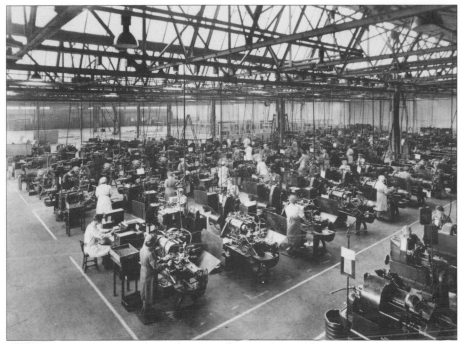

Machine Shop at Hillington during the War

Merlin engine installed in a Spitfire

factory blocks and 1800 jobs but William Miller had other plans up his sleeve. By the time Rolls-Royce had assumed full responsibility for the Scottish factories in 1947, they were employing 4200 people. With the Cold War in place, another major conflict breaking out in Korea, there were contracts to re-quip the RAF with Avon jet engines – and within ten years the company had expanded from Hillington to factories at Blantyre, Larkhall, Cardonald and East Kilbride, which became Scotland's first wholly jet-engine factory.

The denouement of this incredible tale was that, by the early 1960s, William Miller had virtually fulfilled his 1945 ambition to restore all 15,000 jobs in Scotland. (His enthusiasm was passed on to his sons, Bill and Eric, later founded Prestwick Circuits).

Rolls-Royce marched on as the byword for excellence. But it all went disastrously wrong when the company undertook to develop the new RB211 engine in an order for the giant Lockheed company of America. It turned to be so costly and time-consuming that Rolls-Royce went bankrupt before being taken into state control in 1971.

The irony was that the development of that engine was perhaps essential to the future of the company. For when it finally reached production it was a notable success.

Meanwhile the name of Miller had taken on an added significance for Rolls-Royce. Another of that name, Stewart Miller from Kirkcaldy, was rising through the company, maintaining that high reputation of Scottish engineers. On his way to the top at Derby as boss of the Aerospace Group, he headed the 1970s project which put the RB211 into the new Boeing 757, taking it right from conceptual stage to the point of carrying passengers.

By the 1990s Stewart Miller could point to the range of Rolls-Royce consumers – 300 airlines and 100 armed forces around the world – and claim that 60 of those airlines were using developments of the RB211 engine.

With all the company's traumas, on top of recession and military cutbacks, the Scottish operation had been severely trimmed since William Miller's success of the 1960s.

But Rolls-Royce has survived in Scotland, the Hillington factory engaged exclusively in the manufacture of compressor blades and other components for the jet engines. East Kilbride looks after the repair and overhaul of aero engines already in service, stripping them down and replacing worn parts.

Down the years it has been involved in developments from the Merlin, Griffon, Derwent and Dart engines to the Avon and Spey and more recently the V2500 and the Tay engine which powered a new family of Gulfstream, the highly

Rolls-Royce design and engineering at East Kilbride – The Rolls-Royce Tay with Keith Bradshaw (Chief Design Engineer), Norman Wilson (formerly Chief Engineer Tay) and Sandy Macfarlane (Manager, Engineering and Experimental, East Kilbride)

successful executive jet. Overhaul of the Pegasus engine for the Harrier Jump Jet was moved from Bristol to East Kilbride.

And into the mid-1990s, Rolls-Royce in Scotland has been working on the successor to the Tay, the engine to power 100-plus-seater planes, which has been developed in conjunction with the BMW company.

So Scotland's part in the great story of Rolls-Royce continues towards a new century, led by people like Aberdonian Sandy Macfarlane, in charge of design and engineering, Colin Smallwood, boss of manufacturing at Hillington, and Jim Taylor, who looks after repair and overhaul at East Kilbride. It is a part which would not have existed but for the efforts of that determined Scot, William Miller, a prophet who, in a manner not unfamiliar, gained little honour in his own land.

International Aero Engines V2500 developed by Rolls-Royce at East Kilbride

FLYING-BOATS FROM THE CLYDE

Denny of Dumbarton had long since established its name as one of the notable shipbuilders on the Clyde, extending its scope with much enterprise to developing one of the earliest helicopters. It had also been contracted to build some aircraft for the Royal Flying Corps in the First World War.

But a whole new chapter opened in 1936 when the threat of war with Hitler's Germany sparked off a re-armament programme, which included the setting up of so-called "shadow" factories all over Britain.

Denny thus cooperated with Blackburn Aircraft Ltd of Brough to set up an aircraft production line on the road leading to Dumbarton Castle. An aircraft-carrying barge was built to transport the completed planes.

A Blackburn Botha at Abbotsinch with a Swordfish in the background

The Blackburn factory was to build a new twin-engined torpedo bomber called the Botha but that turned out to be badly under powered and was never operational, written off as one of the failure's of the war.

That disappointment was more than made good, however, by the success which attended the Short Sunderland flying-boats which were built at Dumbarton and became widely acclaimed for their design and craftsmanship.

The RAF desperately needed those machines to counter the menace of the German U-boats. The site of the factory was chosen for its direct access to the Clyde for launch and transport and the slipway to accommodate the Sunderland was built in 1939.

In the period from November 1941 until the end of the war in 1945, a total of 242 flying boats were built in the shadow of the rock. At the peak of production one Sunderland was turned out every three days, the construction time from laying the keel to launch amounting to 51 days.

When the first of the Sunderlands was launched the roar of the Pegasus engine brought Blackburn workers excitedly to the scene to witness their aircraft on its way. There was much local pride in what had been achieved.

At first the flying-boats were towed by barge down the Clyde before permission was granted to fly them off directly from the Blackburn launching site.

A Blackburn-built Sunderland makes a low pass over the Clyde at Dumbarton Rock

As with many more of those wartime enterprises, of course, the need for the product came to an end in 1945. Blackburn went over to the production of aluminium houses, which helped to meet the post-war scarcity of accommodation – and two streetfuls of them in Dumbarton were named Blackburn Crescent and Sunderland Avenue.

But that was overtaken in time by conventional housing and the Blackburn factory, with its fine record of wartime activity, closed down for good in 1960.

The way in which Scotland's weekend flyers of the 1930s became daring airmen in the Battle of Britain – and extended the comradeship of the skies to the enemy they sought to destroy – comes alive as powerful drama when you examine the story of the Auxiliary Air Force.

The whole idea had arisen at the end of the First World War when Marshal of the Royal Air Force Hugh Trenchard saw the need to keep a good quality reserve of "Territorial" airmen, a kind of corps d'elite, a wise thought which helped save Britain from Hitler's tyranny.

The first four auxiliary squadrons, formed in 1925, included No. 602 (City of Glasgow) and No. 603 (City of Edinburgh), creating a healthy rivalry which ensured the highest standard of operation. A third Scottish squadron was formed some years later as No. 612 (County of Aberdeen).

The City of Glasgow Squadron, the first in existence, was formed officially on 15 September 1925, a significant date which would also be declared Battle of Britain Day in 1940.

The Glasgow men were to gain much reflected glory in 1933 when two of their distinguished pilots, the Marquis of Clydesdale and David McIntyre, became the first human beings to look down on the summit of Mount Everest.

But it was naturally the Second World War which brought all those weekend air crews into their own, the Glasgow men by now flying from Abbotsinch and the Edinburgh men from Turnhouse.

On 3 September 1939 Prime Minister Neville Chamberlain had no sooner finished his broadcast, declaring war on Germany, than the citizens of Edinburgh heard the local Spitfires taking their place overhead in the front-line defence of the United Kingdom .

A year later that squadron would go south to RAF Hornchurch, near London, from which it would play a noble part in the Battle of Britain, under Squadron Leader George Denholm.

Meanwhile the City of Glasgow, under Squadron Leader Sandy Johnstone (he has written the foreword to this book) headed for Westhampnett, on the south coast of England near Chichester, to join in that same epic battle of the air against the might of the Luftwaffe, all those men becoming immortalised in Winston Churchill's words as part of "The Few," to whom so much was owed by so many.

There were impressive statistics of enemy planes destroyed, brave deeds rewarded and, sadly, a tragic toll of those who did not survive. But, for all the heroics of the Battle of Britain, Scotland's auxiliary squadrons reserved some of their finest moments for action over the home territory. That included the first air action over Britain, involving both the Edinburgh and Glasgow squadrons.

Between sorties at Drem on 16 October 1939. 602 Squadron pilots Finlay Boyd, George Pinkerton, Sandy Johnstone, Paul Webb, Alastair Grant and Nigel Graeme

The frontline would be on the east coast, nearer Germany, so No. 602 Squadron moved across from Glasgow to be based at Drem, near North Berwick in East Lothian.

For both squadrons the war came alive on 16 October 1939 when nine Junkers 88s long-range dive-bombers of KG30 came flying in from the German island of Sylt, near Denmark, to attack shipping in the Firth of Forth, the Rosyth Dockyard and the Forth Bridge.

It was an afternoon raid – the first time the Spitfire had ever been in action against the Germans – and thousands of people in Edinburgh went into the streets to gaze upwards. With no air-raid warning sounding, however, they believed it to be a large-scale practice. Then a tramcar travelling through Portobello was struck by shrapnel and that was the starting point of a complaint later lodged with the Chief Constable of Midlothian, who was responsible for the warning system.

The reality was that a fierce battle was raging over the Forth, in which the Germans were routed by the Scots, who shot down two of their planes into the sea and damed another. From Glasgow, George Pinkerton and Archie McKellar thought they had claimed the first enemy aircraft of the war but a similar claim came from the Edinburgh men, on behalf of Patrick Gifford, the Procurator-Fiscal of Castle Douglas. Something of an argument developed but when the timings were investigated Gifford gave more precise details and, by a few minutes over Pinkerton, the farmer from Houston, Renfrewshire, he was declared to have been the first pilot to shoot down a German raider in the war over the UK.

One of the survivors plucked from the sea turned out to be the leader of the raid, Hauptmann Helmut Pohle – and the subsequent events reveal truths about the human spirit which outstrip the importance of records.

Pat Gifford of 603 Squadron at Turnhouse in October 1939 By then equipped with Spitfires, the Squadron still had some of its earlier Gladiators which can be seen in the background

The unconscious Pohle landed in the military hospital at Edinburgh Castle and, when he came to his senses, the two special visitors bringing particular comfort to his bedside were none other than Pat Gifford and George Pinkerton, the Scots who had just been knocking hell out of his German squadron!

Pinkerton followed up with a letter to Pohle, hoping he was now on the road to a speedy recovery and adding these moving sentiments: "We are at war but that fact does not prevent me from acknowledging the very gallant fight which you put up. These sweets and cigarettes which I ask you to accept are an evidence of my good wishes to you and of my hope that in due course you will have a happy reunion with your people at home."

Helmut Pohle later wrote his appreciation of the medical care he received. Though he had doubted a rather primitive method of straightening his damaged teeth (he put it down to Scottish thriftiness!) he had to admit that, 46 years later, they were standing upright in perfect condition.

He remembered the visit of Patrick Gifford, whom he saw as "the presentation of a nice young officer of the Royal Air Force. I am violently shaken to hear of the death of Fl.Lt. Gifford in May 1940."

Having returned thanks for Pinkerton's sweets and good wishes, "in old airman comradeship," he had kept up a post-war connection and knew that George returned to farming in Renfrewshire, just as Helmut himself was now a farmer by the Baltic Sea, 40 miles north of Lubeck – both suffering from the Common Agricultural Policies of the European Union, he said!

Pinkerton and Gifford both received the DFC for their bravery. But if these human contacts show up the underlying folly of war, the matter is just as delicately portrayed by the funeral which Scotland gave to two of Pohle's young airmen who did not have his luck of survival.

As their leader lay in hospital, they were taken to Portobello Cemetery, where the public turned out in large numbers and in silent respect, also wondering if the German Air Force might attempt to drop a wreath, as was done by both sides in the First World War. It didn't happen. Men of the RAF carried the coffins to the graveside and the Rev. Rossie Brown of Murrayfield Church led the burial service.

With much dignity, he included these words: "It is without any hostility or hatred in our hearts against any people that we lay these two young airmen to their rest. It is, on the contrary, with goodwill towards all and genuine desire for kind and brotherly relations with them.

"The obsequies in which we are now engaged are further a tribute to the faithfulness in duty of those two young Germans, whereby they fought fairly and died bravely, and an expression of our Christian hope that in another world than this they will find the peace denied to them on earth, fruition of the manhood hardly as yet in flower. God give us the loyalty and devotion to our country and cause which they have shown to theirs. God rest their souls; and may He who knows the tenderness of the tie which binds us to our own sustain and comfort those who love them."

As to that action over the Forth, Helmut Pohle threw some fresh light on the reason for the raid. They had come, he said, to attack HMS Hood, in her day the biggest warship in the world, which was apparently heading for Rosyth that morning.

His orders were to attack her only if she were at sea but strictly not in port because Germany was still hopeful of a peace settlement with Britain and didn't want to risk civilian casualties.

What they thought was the Hood, which would later meet a ghastly fate at the hands of the dreaded Bismarck, had reached port so Pohle and his airmen turned their attention instead to HMS Southampton and HMS Edinburgh.

But if those Germans came down in the sea, the first plane to be brought down on land in the Second World War fell to 602 Squadron's Archie McKellar who, on 28 November 1939, spotted a Heinkel over North Berwick, waded in with all guns blazing and and brought it down in a field near Haddington.

Those auxiliary squadrons continued to give sterling service throughout the war, from Normandy and Northern Europe to attacking the sites of those deadly German rockets. They were disbanded at the end of the war but revived in 1946 for a post-war life which extended until 1957 when the flying squadrons were closed down.

If there is much emotion, tragedy and triumph in these real-life tales of war in the air, there was occasionally a glimmer of humour to lighten the burden. In February 1940, the commanding officer of 602 Squadron, Douglas Farquhar, was leading a section which included the only cannon-armed Spitfire in the RAF. He was intercepting a Heinkel off the Scottish coast and had silenced the rear gunner when he decided to call in the special aircraft to show what it could do. He stood off to watch as the cannons did their job and the German raider went down on a stretch of land near St Abb's Head.

Keen to see what damage had been down, Farquhar thought he would land his Spitfire alongside the German, who had managed to make a successful wheels-up landing. But the victor was not so lucky. He came down in a bog and turned over, to find himself trapped inside and suspended by his harness.

Having set fire to their own plane, the crew of the Heinkel very sportingly came across to rescue the red-faced Scot, lifting the Spitfire so that he could crawl out and restore some dignity.

He was given a ticking-off by his superiors, who didn't have quite the sense of humour of King George VI when he visited the squadron at Drem a few weeks later.

Farquhar was due to receive a Distinguished Flying Cross and when His Majesty heard the story, he couldn't contain his amusement!

Having already decorated Sqn Ldr A D Farquhar with the DFC, HM King George VI meets other members of 602 Squadron at Drem during his visit on 26 February 1940

Flight Lieutenant George Pinkerton of 602 Squadron's 'B' Flight in Spitfire Ia, L1019 'LO–S' "Grumpy", attacking a Ju88 of KG30 over the Firth of Forth near Crail just before 3·00pm. Pinkerton had also been in action on the morning of 16 October when he damaged a lone He111 of KG26 which was on a reconnaissance mission

Flight Lieutenant Pat Gifford of 603 Squadron's Red section in Spitfire Ia, L1070 'XT–A' "Stickleback", over the Firth of Forth near Port Seton. Gifford was first to shoot down a Ju88 of KG30 making his 'kill' at around 2·30 to 3·00pm on 16 October 1939

THE ATLANTIC FERRY

The Americans had not yet entered the Second World War in 1940 but they were helping to supply the Royal Air Force with much-needed aircraft. Lockheed Hudsons were being transported across the Atlantic on British ships, though German U-boats were scoring successes against our fleet.

When Winston Churchill became Prime Minister that year he immediately appointed Lord Beaverbrook, dynamic owner of the Daily Express, to be his Minister of Aircraft Production. He, in turn, struck on the idea of flying the planes to Britain, even if transatlantic flight was still very much in its infancy.

They would fly from Lockheed's factory in California to a dispatch point in Canada to begin what would come to be known as the Atlantic Air Ferry.

The first formation of planes left Gander, Newfoundland, on 10 November 1940 and arrived next day at the British destination, which was to be Aldergrove Airport, Belfast. Later that month another consignment was heading for Britain when one of the Hudsons lost contact with the others and came in to land at Prestwick instead. It took the duty officer some time to focus on the fact that Captain Pat Eves had just flown the Atlantic.

Yet out of this extraordinary mischance, Prestwick Airport, with its fog-free record and reputation, was then chosen to replace Aldergrove as the British destination.

By the time the war ended in 1945, this "bridge" across the Atlantic would involve Prestwick in no fewer than 37,000 flights! At first the air crews went back to Canada by ship but this slowed up the merry-go-round of delivery. The answer would be to fly them back but that east-west journey across the Atlantic, with its fierce headwinds, was still a treacherous business, underlining the feat of Scotland's Jim Mollison in 1933, as described in another chapter.

But it would have to be tried. So six Liberator bombers were converted in the summer of 1941 and captains from BOAC, engaged to keep the service going, thus brought in the first-ever east-west winter crossing of the Atlantic.

For those passenger pilots it was an uncomfortable journey, unpressurised, with mattresses to cushion the worst of the bumps, gloves to keep warm and a ration of oxygen from small bottles.

So Prestwick became a busy place, with as many as 300 planes coming in on a single day, with 23 types including Flying Fortresses, Dakotas and Mosquitoes.

Intertwined with the wartime security of this bustle came Commonwealth Prime Ministers, atomic scientists, famous entertainers and members of the Royal Family, like the Duke of Kent, who was not alone in travelling under an assumed name.

Out of it all Prestwick gained a 6,600ft runway, 300 feet wide, and the Transatlantic Air Control Centre was moved north from Gloucester.

Once those planes arrived from North America, of course, they had to be flown on to maintenance bases throughout the country to have their military equipment installed before joining the squadrons.

That delivery service was the task of the Air Transport Auxiliary (ATA), in which women took their place alongside the men as pilots and flight engineers. Those ladies included the legendary solo flyer Amy Johnson, who was on a trip south from Prestwick in 1941 when she perished in the Thames Estuary.
Under Group Captain David McIntyre, virtually the father of its airport, Prestwick made the most of the wartime opportunity and showed what would surely now be possible by way of transatlantic travel in the post-war world.

The Hudson Mk.3, T9426, which 'inaugurated' the Atlantic Ferry service to Prestwick.
The aircraft, flown by Captain E P M Eves, touched down at 11.40 am GMT
on 28 November 1940

FERRANTI IN AVIATION

If the Scots had done no more than develop and build aircraft, pioneer services and send brave flyers into the sky their contribution to the story of aviation would still have been substantial.

But it takes on a deeper dimension when you consider the part played by Ferranti of Edinburgh in creating the scientific instruments which have brought flying to the sophisticated levels of today.

From the wonders of radar to the delicate instruments of Concorde and the incredibly accurate equipment which played a vital part in both the Falkland and Gulf Wars, Scotland has given the world some of its best technology.

The Ferranti story began with the remarkable Sebastian de Ferranti, a Liverpool boy of Italian extraction, who became an inventor of such skill and scope that he registered more than 400 patents ranging from steam turbines to bicycle tyres. By 1887 he had created the world's first high-voltage power station at Deptford, London. And he was only 23 years of age.

On his death in 1930 Ferranti was succeeded by his son and the company was now building up an instrument department at Hollinwood in Lancashire, with a particular eye on the aircraft industry.

Into the Second World War that department was asked by the Ministry of Aircraft Production to help develop a new device called the Gyro Gun Sight. This could shorten the war so the matter was urgent. But Ferranti's plant at Hollinwood was at full stretch and they had to look elsewhere for space and available workers.

Edinburgh was the choice and after considering various buildings, including Portobello ice-rink, Ferranti decided to build from scratch at Crewe Toll on Ferry Road. The man appointed as Edinburgh manager was John Toothill, who had joined the company as chief cost accountant in 1935 and would come to be described as the father of Scotland's electronic industry.

The factory was ready in 18 weeks and the significance of what was happening at Ferranti (and some "daughter" companies like Barr and Stroud) was revealed when the Daily Express reported in 1944 that "Luftwaffe leaders have been perplexed at the extraordinary success of RAF planes in shooting down machines of their squadrons. Today the secret is out. The RAF have been using a new gunsight....one of Britain's greatest scientific achievements." It was later hailed as perhaps the single most important piece of equipment introduced into service during the war.

By August 1945 the Edinburgh factory had produced nearly 10,000 of those gunsights but now that the war was over there was no more need for them. With Edinburgh facing closure, Sir Vincent de Ferranti offered to retain the works on condition it could pay its way.

John Toothill searched for means of survival and came up with everything from cooker switches and surgical knives to a slide projector for children, produced in collaboration with Enid Blyton.

Research into high technology continued, however, geared very much to the aircraft instruments which would surely be needed in the post-war growth of civil air traffic.

The father of radar, distinguished Scotsman Sir Robert Watson-Watt, helped the company gain a development contract for distance measuring equipment and the Ministry of Supply provided a Dakota aircraft to support the trials.

That was followed by a Sea Fury which joined the new Ferranti Flying Unit at Turnhouse and provided information for the attack systems of aircraft being proposed for the Royal Navy. It was used to attack a target near North Berwick. Sadly, in September 1953 the pilot of the Sea Fury, Dougie Shaw, and a ground crew member went on a project sortie and were killed when the plane crashed at Longniddry.

Sir John Toothill (centre) looks on as Sebastian de Ferranti (right) receives the 1967 Queen's Award for Industry from Edinburgh's Lord Provost.

Already using computer-controlled machinery, Ferranti was pulling in multi-million pound orders. But because of the secret nature of so much of the work, it was unable to reveal, even to its own shareholders, the level of success.

The Ferranti achievements were recognised, however, when John Toothill was awarded the CBE in 1955 and then knighted. He also became the author of the famous Toothill Report on industry location and employment, regarded as the most important policy document since the Beveridge Report of 1944

When Ferranti decided to replace a de Havilland Dove with a Heron, the chosen plane was found to have been the personal transport of Dr Konrad Adenauer, the Chancellor West Germany. Before it arrived in Scotland, the Iron Crosses were hastily painted out!

Into the 1960s and orders worth tens of millions were pouring in for the Bloodhound Guided Missile system. But it is when you are riding high that minor embarrassments can arise. When Sir Vincent de Ferranti came to open the Silverknowes laboratory complex in 1961, he pressed the button to unveil the plaque – but the curtain didn't open! The company at the high end of technology blushed at such an elementary failure – but proceeded to open up the new facility so that the families could see round it. Such was the secrecy of some of the work that scientific workers were said to have paid a visit to find out exactly what they were working on!

Ferranti was developing projects like a moving map display, which could give air crews a view of the whole of Europe on a screen. And John Toothill was proudly leading a visit to Sud Aviation at Toulouse, the French partner in Concorde, which was glad to show off its Ferranti equipment.

By 1968 Ferranti was the biggest single employer in Scotland, with 6,600

Dakota TS423 with modified nose at Turnhouse

Though Ferranti was still expanding, with 7,500 employees stretching from Edinburgh, Livingston and Bellshill to Dundee and Aberdeen, the Government body which had taken a 50% stake in the company announced it was pulling out of the investment. This set off an early warning that it could fall victim to a takeover.

Attention was diverted by the Falklands War of 1982 in which Ferranti target equipment aided the accurate attacks on Stanley airfield. There were even company employees aboard the Task Force ships and one engineer, Dave McAlpine, who was on HMS Hermes, was awarded the MBE for his work.

Indeed, Ferranti played a part in the Argentinian surrender at Port Stanley. Such was the accuracy of targeting that a broadcast telling the demoralised Argentines that their headquarters was next on the list persuaded them to give in just 10 minutes before the plane was due.

Into the 1990s and the Gulf War brought the Edinburgh company into prominence once more. Again the highly sophisticated instruments helped Tornado crews to score direct hits on Iraqi aircraft shelters.

Ferranti personnel flew from Edinburgh to Tabuk to give their expert support throughout the war.

Before this, however, the company had surprised the City with news that it was merging with International Signal and Control, whose founder, a certain James Guerin, said it combined technical excellence with selling expertise and would give access to world-wide markets.

Then in May 1989 Mr Guerin left Ferranti International and four months later the shares were suspended. Irregularities had come to light and it was announced that Ferranti had been defrauded by James Guerin to the tune of £215 million.

The future was now quite definitely in the balance and in March 1990 Ferranti International was sold for £310 million to GEC, one of its main competitors over the years, which had now acquired the expertise of Scotland's leading electronics company.

It became a subsidiary of GEC Marconi. With company morale at an all-time

This Sea Fury T20 was a replacement for the machine which crashed. In the cockpits are A E Featherstone and Peter Gibson

people. It was also gaining the contract for the microwave link for radar at Prestwick Airport. As this triumph of high technology continued, even breaking into the Japanese aircraft market, there was success on a rather different plain. The company's football team, Ferranti Thistle, won a place in the Second Division of the Scottish League, a unique achievement for a works team in British football history. Later gaining promotion to the First Division, it had however a name which was too commercial for the powers-that-be and Ferranti Thistle became Meadowbank Thistle, after the Edinburgh stadium where they played.

The recession of 1974, with its three-day week, was partly responsible for a hitch in Ferranti's fortunes and some speculation about its future. Four years later it went for a Stock Exchange listing.

low, they did at least land the £300 million contract for the much-publicised European Fighter Aircraft. But there were more and more labour cutbacks and closures.

The final blow to local pride came in 1993 when all GEC Marconi avionics companies were merged under a name which did not include the famous name of Ferranti.

Thus one of Scotland's greatest industrial success stories reached the 50th anniversary of its opening in Edinburgh without "Ferranti" on the original Crewe Toll factory.

The only constant factor in life may be change but too often it seems that a small nation like Scotland comes out of it on the wrong side.

Three of the Ferranti Flying Unit's Canberra B(I)8s seen at Turnhouse in the early 1960s. These aircraft were used on trials of the AI 23 AIRPASS radar which equipped the Lightning interceptor.

Canberra B(I)8, WJ643, with modified nose housing Laser Ranger and Marked Target Seeker equipment which was subsequently installed in the Jaguar, Harrier and Tornado aircraft. The pilot, Len Houston, is seen with a Ferranti technician.

In addition to eight Canberras, the Ferranti Flying Unit also operated a Buccaneer S1, Varsity, Valetta, Vampire FT5, Wyvern, Sea Fury, Dakota, Hunter, 2 Gannets and a selection of Meteors one of which, the NF14, was subsequently presented to the Museum of Flight at East Fortune.

THE MYSTERY OF HESS

The most bizarre adventure to cross the pages of aviation history in Scotland came to light on the Saturday night of 10 May 1941 when, at the height of the world war with Nazi Germany, a Messerschmitt 110 aeroplane crash-landed in a field at Eaglesham, just south of Glasgow. The pilot who hirpled away with a broken ankle turned out to be none other than Adolf Hitler's own deputy, Rudolf Hess.

It was the stuff of unlikely fiction and indeed there are those who produce theories suggesting it was all a conspiracy and that the pilot was really a lookalike standing in for Hess.

Having met some of those propagating the theories, however, I came to suspect the power of fertile imagination.

The subsequent story was that the man who came down at Floors Farm, Eaglesham, was the same man later produced at the Nuremberg Trials of 1946, seated alongside the other Nazi criminals who seemed to recognise him as the Rudolf Hess they knew. And the visits from his wife and son in later years brought forth no denials that he was the real man.

Spared the gallows, he spent the rest of his life in Spandau Jail, Berlin, and died there in 1987, aged 93. Again there were questions as to whether he hanged himself or was murdered.

So what was it all about? The political background was that there were people in Germany (and not a few in Britain) who thought the two countries should really be lining up together against the Soviet Union. They included Rudolf Hess, who obtained a list of influential British people from Albrecht Haushofer, the son of Hess's university tutor, who happened to be a friend of the Duke of Hamilton (the one who made the historic flight over Everest, described in this book).

Whether acting as peacemaker on his own we shall never know – his flight seems to have been a genuine surprise to Hitler – but the fact is that he came down on that farmer's field at Eaglesham, to be rounded up and taken to a farmhouse by a local ploughman, David McLean.

At first giving his name as Hauptmann Alfred Horn, he asked to be taken to the Duke of Hamilton. He had apparently run short of fuel in seeking out the Duke's Lanarkshire home at Dungavel House.

Later identifying himself as Rudolf Hess, he was taken to Buchanan Castle military hospital and Maryhill Barracks, Glasgow, where his guards included Willie Ross, a future Secretary of State for Scotland, and Bob Shaw, who became a distinguished professor at Strathclyde University.

He told Shaw he was on a reconnaissance flight in a plane provided by his friend Willi Messerschmitt. Hess was of course a well-known pilot from pre-war days, having won the 1934 air race round Germany's highest mountain, the Zugspitze.

The two men summoned to question him were the Duke of Hamilton, whom he claimed to have met at the Berlin Olympics of 1936, and Ivone Kirkpatrick, a former official at the British Embassy in Berlin.

The Duke went hotfoot next day to report to Winston Churchill, who was spending the weekend at Ditchley Park, Oxfordshire. The Prime Minister is reported to have said "Hess or no Hess, I'm going to see the Marx Brothers!" He did – and then got down to hearing the full story.

How the people of Scotland read about the event

But Churchill was having none of the German's peace proposals and the Deputy Fuhrer became a prisoner, with a spell in the Tower of London, before finally being delivered to the Nuremberg war trials.

Churchill surprised some by playing down the propaganda aspect of Hess's flight but there was perhaps good reason. There were hints of our own Secret Intelligence Service having something to do with it. And, in encouraging the Americans into the war, the Prime Minister wouldn't want them to know that the German view, however erroneous, of who might be interested in making peace included such prominent names as Alec Douglas-Home, future Prime Minister who was with Chamberlain at the Munich talks with Hitler, R A Butler, Churchill's future Chancellor, Lord Halifax, Sir Samuel Hoare and the Hon J J Astor, owner of The Times.

So Hess went to Spandau for the rest of his life and, in the 1960s, with friends in influential places, I came nearer than the law permitted to observing him at close quarters. It didn't quite come off however!

The arguments began to rage. Among those casting doubts on the identity of the German pilot was someone who did have close contact in Spandau, army surgeon Hugh Thomas, who told me he had examined the prisoner and found no trace of a lung wound which the real Hess sustained in the First World War. He said it should have shown.

Then the plane on which he left Augsburg that Saturday of 1941 was evidently not the one which crashed at Eaglesham some hours later. Some say he changed planes at Aalborg in Denmark, where Messerschmitts were based.

This is not the place to explore the multitude of theories. Enough to say that that German aeroplane coming out of the night sky over Eaglesham in 1941 provided one of the strangest tales in the history of aviation.

Whether the man at the controls was really Hitler's deputy will be raked over as one of the lingering mysteries. My own humble view is that the man was Rudolf Hess.

My fragmented aviation memories of 1941
by D Cameron McNicol

The Heinkels droned incessantly overhead for hour after hour throughout the night, straight down the Leven Valley from Loch Lomond. We were sitting in a brick built shelter as someone said "No good for a direct hit but it helps against the blast!"

For an eight year old, all eyes and ears, my only comment was "Be quiet – the pilots might hear you and drop their bombs". Why did those grown-ups not listen to me? Why did they go on singing that funny old song *We're gonna Hang Out Our Washing on the Siegfried Line?*

We were all out of the tenement and in the shelter except Mrs Macgregor. Nobody and certainly not German planes overhead would move her.

Next morning the cemetery had been hit, shining as it did in the moonlight with reflections off the gravestones. Bridge Street had been strafed and fires had raged on the hillside by the Pappert Well but the real damage had been done in Clydebank – the Holy City no more – and they came back the next night for another go.

Result – 6 months off school to let the people of Clydebank live in our classrooms; watching the Lysanders purr overhead and the Spitfires and Hurricanes preparing for dog fights; climbing Carman and over to Rhu to see the Sunderlands heaving through the waters of the Clyde from the Flying Boat Station.

LADY MACROBERT'S REPLY

ew stories of human grit and courage can surpass that of Lady MacRobert of Douneside estate at Tarland in Aberdeenshire, who carved her own distinctive niche in aviation history during the Second World War.

She was the widow who, having brought up her three young sons, had already lost the eldest, Alasdair, in a flying accident just before the war. Now the second boy, Roderic, was off to the Royal Air Force and piloting a highly effective Hurricane raid on German positions in the Middle East when he wheeled away for home and was shot down.

So, just a fortnight after his 26th birthday, another MacRobert life was ended. On hearing of his bravery, his mother steeled herself to say: "I'm proud to think that Roderic did his duty and carried out so well the spirit of our family motto: Glory is the reward of valour."

Her only remaining son, Iain, was already serving as a pilot with Coastal Command when he heard of his brother's death in May 1941. He was given leave and returned to his mother at Douneside. But duty called and he was back in the cockpit when, in the following month, the unthinkable happened.

The last of the MacRoberts was lost while searching for a bomber crew said to be in a dinghy somewhere in the North Sea.

How do you explain the courage of a woman who then sat down and wrote to Sir Archibald Sinclair, Secretary of State for Air: "It is my wish to make a mother's immediate reply, in the way that I know would also be my boys' reply, attacking, striking sharply.... It is with a mother's pride that I enclose a cheque for £25,000 to buy a bomber to carry out their work in the most effective way. This expresses my reaction on receiving the news about my sons.

"They would be glad that their mother replied for them and helped to strike a blow at the enemy. So I feel that a suitable name for the bomber would be 'MacRobert's Reply.' With my cheque goes my sympathy to those mothers who have also lost sons, and gratitude to all other mothers whose sons so gallantly carry on the fight."

The Stirling bomber was handed over to Flying Officer P J S Boggis from Dumfriesshire, who captained most of its 12 operational missions, including a raid on German ships at Brest, for which he received the DFC. MacRobert's Reply also flew from Lossiemouth to attack the infamous Tirpitz in a Norwegian fjord.

Lady MacRobert followed up her gesture with another gift of £25,000 to buy four Hurricanes, three of which were named after her sons while the fourth was called 'MacRobert's Salute to Russia.'

The wealthy background of these gifts was no more than a generation deep. It began with the father of those three pilots, Alexander MacRobert, a working-class boy from Aberdeen who left school at 14 and joined the Stoneywood paperworks, where his father was a labourer.

Studying at evening classes, he sought a better future in India, emigrating in 1884 to work in a woollen mill which was struggling. The young Aberdonian

Fg Off Peter Boggis in the Stirling I, N6086 'LS–F', presented to the RAF and allocated to XV Squadron on 15 September 1941 bearing the MacRobert's family crest on the nose

The cheque for £25,000 to buy the Hurricanes

became manager and not only saved the business but rose to be a leader of industry in the sub-continent.

He returned to be honoured by Aberdeen University and to buy Douneside estate as a retirement home for his parents. Tragically, his Aberdonian wife, Georgina Porter, died of cancer and MacRobert was inconsolable.

By the time he received a knighthood and a baronetcy, he had met and married Rachel Workman, daughter of the redoubtable American mountaineer, Fanny Bullock Workman.

By then he was 57 (Rachel was 30 years younger) and belatedly became the father of the three boys who would write their names into flying history. His crowning business achievement was to amalgamate the textile industry into the huge British India Corporation.

When he died suddenly at Douneside in 1922, the title passed to 10-year-old Alasdair, who eventually became chairman of the Corporation. He was also developing aviation in India when, just before his 27th birthday in 1938, he was killed in a flying accident near Luton.

It was the start of the MacRobert tragedy. Lady MacRobert inherited money from her American background and in 1943 established the family trust which has given massive support to worthy causes.

Typical of the recipients was Stirling University which was given £250,000 to create the MacRobert Centre. The former House of Cromar at Douneside, re-named Alastrean to suggest the names of her sons, was Lady MacRobert's gift as a home for former RAF personnel, still active today.

In 1993 the campaign to set up a children's hospice in Scotland received £2 million from the trust, the largest single donation ever received by a Scottish charity.

The powerful personality of Lady MacRobert touched on many lives, not least those of airmen returning from the Second World War. She helped to educate them and gave them jobs.

People like Bill Reid VC, mentioned elsewhere in this book, was one of those who found a successful career in her farming operation. Now retired in Crieff, Bill observed: "She liked to have young airmen around her. I think there was something in the idea that we were the substitute sons."

Lady MacRobert died at Douneside in September 1954 and is buried in a tree-sheltered spot by the beautiful lawns. She was the last link in a remarkable tale of one family's skill, determination, public service and, above all, courage.

Lady MacRobert with her three sons

XV Squadron's Tornado GR1 "MacRobert's Reply" complete with MacRobert tartan fin band and family crest on the nose

THE BALL-BEARING RUN

So many fronts demanded public attention during the Second World War – and so much had to be kept secret – that many a drama was enacted beneath our very noses of which we knew little or nothing.

British Overseas Airways had retained its civilian link with Scandinavia after the outbreak of war but the plane warming up at Perth for the regular crossing to Stockholm on 9 April 1940 was suddenly withdrawn. Why? The big headlines that morning announced Hitler's invasion of Norway and Denmark and two of the British planes were already stranded in the wrong place.

One had to be surrendered to the Germans in Oslo but the crew escaped to Stockholm and hitched a lift home in the other one. The traffic officer at Stavanger made his way across the North Sea in a little fishing boat!

Sweden was still a neutral country and Britain had to maintain that link, if only to counteract the Nazi propaganda there. The only way to carry in newspapers and magazines – and the diplomats who would try to persuade the Swedes that Britain was still determined to win the war – was by air.

But there was another pressing reason for keeping that connection with the Swedes. They made some of the finest ball-bearings in the world and, however little that may mean to the uninitiated, that commodity was absolutely vital to the mechanical side of winning a war.

So at the beginning of 1941 BOAC was asked to resume its service from Scotland to Stockholm, a tall order considering the pilots would have to fly unarmed and dangerously close to Germany's powerful anti-aircraft posts. Flying to a backcloth of clear summer skies, moonlight or even the Northern Lights, they soon became accustomed to the hazard of searchlights and anti-aircraft fire.

Even when they reached Stockholm they found themselves with a cautious welcome from wary Swedes, until their nonchalance, courage and regular appearances began to commend them to the locals. The danger in what they were doing came clear from the casualties on the route including Captain L A Wilkins, who had given devoted service in maintaining it.

Leuchars became the Scottish base and various types of planes were used. But it was the introduction of the civilianised de Havilland Mosquito in 1943, with its speed and greater safety, which made all the difference to getting the newspapers and mail to Sweden and those precious ball-bearings back to Britain. As a small plane, the Mosquito carried the ball-bearings in the bomb-bays and had room in the cabin for no more than two men. That was why the next request presented a serious problem.

The Germans were trying to block off Britain's supply of ball-bearings and divert it to themselves so the Air Ministry had an urgent need to fly two elderly gentlemen to Stockholm immediately. They were executives from that particular industry who were going to see what they could do to thwart the Nazi move.

With no room in the cabin, there was only one solution: Strap the visitors in the bomb-bays, little compartments hardly big enough for a man – and opening downwards from the under-belly of the plane.

They were fixed up with a light so that they could read and an intercom link with the pilot but there was no access to the cabin. Equipped with sandwiches and a flask of coffee each, they settled down for this bizarre trip in circumstances which would have driven the claustrophobic insane.

But their mission was vital to the war effort – and it succeeded. So much so that this method of transport was used for other passengers going from Leuchars to Stockholm. But the dangers were still there.

BOAC Mosquito VI G–AGGG coming in to land in the UK

Captain Gilbert Rae was returning to Scotland one moonlit night in July 1943, with one such passenger strapped beneath, when he was attacked yet again by German fighters. From 23,000 feet he dived and twisted towards sea-level, making a remarkable escape from his German pursuers. But the exercise had been so violent and bewildering that his radio officer was buffeted around the cabin to the extent that he needed a fortnight to recover from his injuries.

And what of the poor chap in the belly of the plane, who must have been wondering what on earth was going on? Captain Rae's attempts to rouse him on the intercom were meeting with no success.

Nature had sent his unorthodox passenger blissfully into unconsciousness, where he remained until released from his frightening little cell at Leuchars. Sadly, the courageous Captain Rae was later to lose his life on that same service.

So the ball-bearing run served its vital purpose in helping to defeat Hitler – and added its own worthy chapter to the story of aviation in Scotland.

Mosquito G AGFV of the type used by BOAC on the Leuchars – Sweden service

Another Scottish/Scandanavian connections the memorial stone at RAF Leuchars in Fife which "commemorates the brotherhood in arms between British and Norwegian airmen who fought from these Northern Shores in World War II"

Light aircraft manufacture in Scotland

Aviation Scotland Ltd at Burnbank in Hamilton re-launched production of their ARV1 Super 2 in 1994 and continue to develop the design. The aircraft is marketed complete as the Opus 280 or in kit form as the 'Highlander'. The company entered a joint venture with Hagfors in Sweden due to lack of UK investment.

The qualities which have enabled Scots people to play a disproportionate part in the progress of mankind revealed themselves not least in the nation's contribution towards victory in the Second World War.

The fact that six of Britain's 32 Victoria Crosses won by airmen came to Scotland was double what might have been expected on a population basis.

That war was only a few years behind us when I first encountered one of those six VCs, then working on the farm estates of Lady MacRobert at Douneside in Aberdeenshire, the courageous woman who lost three sons in the air.

But it was much later before I appreciated the full worth of William Reid, the blacksmith's son from Baillieston, Glasgow, who became a wartime legend at the age of 21.

From Coatbridge High School, Bill Reid joined the RAF at 19 and was soon trained as a pilot who would take part in 33 bombing raids over Germany. On the tenth of those adventures he came face to face with the drama which would bring him the Victoria Cross.

William Reid

Heading for Dusseldorf that November night of 1943, his Lancaster was attacked by a Messerschmitt which shattered his windscreen and wounded him in the head. Regaining control of the plane (and feeling the taste of blood in his mouth) Reid found himself under a second attack which killed his navigator and left his wireless operator dying.

But there was no turning back. Somehow he willed that crippled plane to its destination, with 220 miles still to go. Now without a navigator but memorising his course, he reached the target for Flight Sergeant Les Rolton to release the bomb load accurately. Then he turned for home, with some guidance from the Pole Star and the Moon.

By now light-headed from loss of blood, he had to cope with the further emergency of the engines cutting out. Lapsing towards unconsciousness, he managed quite miraculously to land his plane on an American air base in Norfolk, slumped over his controls.

As if that weren't enough, Bill Reid was back attacking a storage tunnel for the dreaded V-2 bombs near Paris when one of our own planes, flying above him released its bombs too soon and struck his Lancaster. He had no option but bale out and find himself under German arrest. As they took him off to prison camp they passed a section of his crashed plane. He asked the guards if he could stop to examine it. Two of his crew lay dead inside as he was marched to captivity with a heavy heart.

Back home in 1945, he studied at Glasgow University and enjoyed a career in agriculture, retiring to Crieff, where he still lives.

The importance of the flying boat in defence was recognised in 1936 with the formation of Coastal Command, a service which destroyed well over 200 submarines and crippled a great many more during the Second World War.

Only one of their four recipients of the VC survived the experience. John Alexander Cruickshank, a former pupil of Aberdeen Grammar School and Daniel Stewart's, Edinburgh, had embarked on a career with the Commercial Bank of Scotland and in 1938 had also joined the Territorial Army.

Called up at the beginning of the war, Cruickshank was still with the Royal Artillery in 1941 when he applied for a transfer to the RAF, gaining his pilot's wings in 1942.

Two years later, qualified as a flying boat pilot and based at Sullom Voe in the Shetlands, he took off with his crew towards the Lofoten Islands, off north-west Norway, on a patrol expected to last upwards of 14 hours. After eight monotonous hours, the crew were preparing for home when they ran into the drama which would bring Cruickshank his Victoria Cross.

Flying low, they spotted a German U-boat and prepared for attack. Zooming in on the vessel, the Catalina's depth charges failed to release. The pilot veered away for a second attack. Shouting "Everybody ready?" Cruickshank came in again. But the Germans were better prepared and an explosion killed the navigator and injured others, including the skipper.

However, Cruickshank stuck to his task and personally released a stick of

John Cruickshank

depth charges which sank U-347. The flying boat and its crew were badly shattered, the main petrol lines were leaking – and they still had five hours' flying to reach Sullom Voe.

Holes in the hull were stopped up and the second pilot took over as another of the crew attended to Cruickshank's wounds in the chest and legs. Drifting several times into and out of unconsciousness, he refused morphia and finally insisted on resuming control.

Collapsing on landing, he needed a blood transfusion and was taken to hospital, where he was found to have no fewer than 72 different wounds, some serious. He received his VC from King George VI at Holyroodhouse, Edinburgh, along with his second pilot, who gained the Distinguished Flying Medal. John Cruickshank returned to banking after the war and eventually retired to Edinburgh.

John Hannah from Paisley had the distinction of being the youngest-ever recipient of the VC for bravery in the air. Son of a Clyde Trust employee, John started as a shoe salesman but joined as an RAF regular just before the war, trained as a wireless operator and was a sergeant at 18.

He was still that age when, during the Battle of Britain in 1940, he took off from Scampton in the cramped conditions of the four-man Hampden to bomb barges in the port of Antwerp, thought to be gathering for a German invasion.

As the plane approached Antwerp it ran into a barrage of anti-aircraft fire and searchlights. The bomb-aimer shouted that his bombs were away but before the pilot could swing clear the aircraft was struck by a shell and became a raging inferno.

Facing the tail, Hannah and the gunner were engulfed in flames, the latter disappearing with his parachute through a hole in the floor. When the navigator wriggled

John Hannah

back to see what was happening, Hannah appeared to be alight and he reckoned the two men were doomed. He then baled out to give the pilot time to follow.

But the burning and suffocating Hannah was fighting the fire on his own back there, using the extinguisher, the flying log book and his flailing hands. Having rescued himself, he crawled forward, a charred spectacle which shocked the pilot. They were now alone. The carrier pigeons had been roasted alive in their basket.

Hannah found the navigator's maps and helped the pilot guide their badly burned plane back to Scampton. Both wing petrol tanks had been torn open but miraculously didn't ignite.

John Hannah from Paisley became a VC at 18, met his future wife but developed tuberculosis and sadly died in 1947.

If it takes moments of crisis to reveal selfless heroism, there was never a better example of it than George Thompson, a ploughman's son from Trinity Gask in Perthshire.

His life might well have been confined to his grocer's job in Kinross but, with the onset of war, he volunteered for the RAF and was eventually accepted for training as a wireless operator.

Victory in Europe was well on the way when young George, flying Lancasters from Bardney in Lincolnshire, was looking forward to the Hogmanay celebrations of 1944. Suddenly the station dance was interrupted by a loudspeaker call to crews. At dawn on New Year's Day they were heading for an attack on the Dortmund-Ems Canal.

On a freezing morning they took off for Germany and were bombing their target when the Lancaster was hit by two shells. Fire raged through the fuselage and George Thompson could see that both turrets were on fire and that the two Welsh gunners were in mortal danger.

Edging past a large hole in the floor, he reached the unconscious Ernie Potts whose flying suit was on fire. With his own clothes now burning, he carried him forward to safety, when one slip would have sent both men hurtling to the ground without a parachute. But Haydn Price was still trapped amid the flames. By now badly burned himself, George Thompson repeated the heroic act.

With the pilot now heading for home the

George Thompson

plane came under further attack and was hirpling badly when a Canadian squadron of Spitfires spotted it and guided it to their own airfield in the Netherlands. The pilot managed to avoid a village as he crash-landed in a field and the fuselage broke up.

As the crew were taken to hospital in Eindhoven, he could hardly believe the burned condition of George Thompson. Sadly, Ernie Potts did not survive the ordeal but Haydn Price lived to have plastic surgery and make a full recovery, owing his life to the courageous Scot.

Thompson was proving a cheerful patient but pneumonia complicated his appalling injuries and he died on 23 January 1945, to be buried in Brussels. The citation for his Victoria Cross paid due tribute to a gallant Scot who risked his life for his comrades - and made the ultimate sacrifice.

Hugh Malcolm from Broughty Ferry decided to make flying his career and entered the RAF College at Cranwell, Lincolnshire, in 1936 when he was 18. Qualified as a pilot and practising for an air display at Manchester in the spring

Hugh Malcolm

of 1939, he came close to losing his life when his Lysander crashed and his injuries included a fractured skull.

He was flying again, however, soon after war broke out and was promoted Flight Lieutenant to a posting at Inverness. He had become a Squadron Leader, flying Blenheims in support of main bombing force raids when, in May 1942, he took part in the first of the 1000–bomber attacks on Cologne. A new design of Blenheim had been supplied when he joined the war in North Africa, based in Algeria, but there were doubts about the plane's suitability.

Malcolm had come under heavy fire when leading attacks on Bizerta airfield and, on 4 December 1942, led another attack on German troop concentrations.

Within an hour of landing he had a message from the army asking for a second aerial operation in the same area. It would mean a daylight attack and there wasn't time to muster fighter support. He knew the danger he faced but decided to respond.

As the Blenheims approached, the Germans signalled the nearest Luftwaffe airfield. No sooner had Malcolm and his men begun to bomb than they were set upon by 50 Messerschmitts in what turned out to be a swift massacre of Allied planes.

Hugh Malcolm's Blenheim was one of the last to be shot down, erupting in flames. Against all the odds, he had shown cool determination and courage – another Scot to receive a posthumous Victoria Cross.

Kenneth Campbell from Saltcoats in Ayrshire gained his own share of immortality in the war against those deadly German battle-cruisers Scharnhorst and Gneisenau, which were about to be joined by the Bismarck, the biggest

warship in the world.

Their mission was to cut off Britain's vital food and war material sealanes in the Atlantic, by which Hitler thought he would starve us into defeat.

Winston Churchill was displeased with the lack of success in countering these vessels and ordered all-out attack if they happened to enter port. His timing was immaculate. That very day the Scharnhorst and Gneisenau were heading into Brest Harbour and a Spitfire reconnaissance photograph showed that the Gneisenau was vulnerable to an aerial torpedo attack.

No. 22 Squadron, with its Bristol Beauforts based near Newquay, Cornwall, received the order and two formations of three took off, one to bomb torpedo nets and the other to carry weapons for the vital attack. They knew the defences around Brest were so massive as to put this adventure into the near-suicidal category.

One of the pilots who would make the killer attack was Ken Campbell, who had started flying while a student at Cambridge before the war. As he came in for his individual attack he dived below 50ft, knowing he had to drop his torpedo as soon as he crossed the breakwater. He released it accurately, pulled into a climb and met the inevitable fury of the German defences. His plane crashed into the harbour.

All four of the crew were buried by the Germans in Brest. Ken Campbell had

Kenneth Campbell

indeed crippled the Gneisenau, which was still undergoing repairs eight months later.

French Resistance workers reported on the bravery of the young Scot and in March 1942 he was awarded a posthumous Victoria Cross, received by his parents from King George VI.

Lancaster B.III of 61 Squadron flown by Bill Reid VC

The periodic dramas of a helicopter snatching survivors from the sea or seeking out victims of the Scottish mountains are the events which focus our attention on Britain's Airborne Search and Rescue service. Sometimes we come to know it more forcibly from tragedies like that on the Piper Alpha oil platform or the horrifying PanAm plane crash at Lockerbie in 1988.

Though it may be taken much for granted at home, the Search and Rescue service is envied by other countries as perhaps the most skilled and effective in the world.

While it was not formalised in the Royal Air Force until 1941, there were air-sea rescues dating back to the First World War. In 1917, for example, a seaplane of the Royal Naval Air Service was trying to rescue the crew of a ditched de Havilland in the North Sea when it ran into difficulties of its own.

A homing pigeon, released with a call for help, collapsed and died as it reached land. But the message was acted upon and six lives were saved. (Pigeon No. 16331 was stuffed and remains a prized exhibit at the RAF Museum at Hendon).

The need for a proper service became vital during the air battles of 1940, when ditched pilots had to depend on their Mae West lifejackets and hope that somebody would pick them up. Too many valuable aircrew lives were being lost.

So the Royal Air Force Search and Rescue was formed and by the end of the war 8,000 airmen were among the 13,000 people who had been saved.

The use of a helicopter to pick up two people off Long Island, New York, in 1945 was a major milestone in the development of air-sea rescue and in Britain the cause was advanced by the Fleet Air Arm, which gained vast experience with the rotary-winged machines.

Until 1994 the control of all these aerial sources was divided between Pitreavie in Fife and Plymouth in Devon, sharing the work north and south of a line from Lowestoft to Aberystwyth. Then it was all centred at Pitreavie, covering an area from the Faroes in the north to the English Channel, eastward across the North Sea and halfway across the Atlantic.

In Scotland the Sea King helicopters are based at Lossiemouth on the Moray Firth and with the Royal Navy at Prestwick and are probably the most effective rescue vehicles to date. They cost well over £3 million to build and more than £4,000 an hour to operate.

At all times a Nimrod maritime patrol aircraft is on standby at RAF Kinloss, not far from Lossiemouth, with the task of flying to the scene of the emergency to coordinate the efforts of helicopters and surface vessels.

The crew of 13 consists of two pilots, two navigators, an engineer and electronics officer and seven electronics operators. Within their array of sophisticated instruments they can mark the spot, locate objects, drop inflatable dinghies and much more.

Scotland's mountain rescue teams are based at Kinloss and Leuchars, each consisting of 35 men, mainly volunteers who come from their various civilian jobs on an unpaid basis. They may be going to look for a missing hill walker or a lost child or heading to a major disaster like Lockerbie.

In 1993, for example, RAF, Royal Navy and HM Coastguard helicopters and mountain rescue teams went to the aid of 1,463 people in distress.

The dependable old Shackletons from Lossiemouth still had a part to play and the rise of the North Sea oil industry has brought the additional help of those helicopters which fly out to the platforms. Companies like Bristow, Bond and British International have weighed in with their widespread experience of those hazardous waters.

A Royal Navy Sea King helicopter from 819 Naval Air Squadron at RNAS Prestwick searches Glen Coe for a missing climber

*Bristows provide and operate specially developed helicopters for
search and rescue operations for the UK's HM Coastguard.
This Sikorsky S-61N Mk.II is recovering a yacht using the 'hi-line' transfer*

*A crewman from an RAF Sea King helicopter is lowered to a fishing boat
in the North Sea*

THOMSON and LOGAN

If the post-war preoccupation with state ownership removed the competitive factor from major industries, it did nothing to dim the pioneering spirit of the Scottish race.

Even in the high-cost, high-risk field of airline operation there were people with vision and courage prepared to take on the big guns. If England could produce a colourful character like Freddie Laker, Scotland had men like Adam Thomson and Willie Logan, names unknown until the 1960s but who would leave their mark on aviation history.

Adam Thomson was the working-class lad from the Cathcart district of Glasgow who walked into a solicitor's office in the city centre one day in 1961 and said "I want to start an airline." It was the stuff of dreams, usually met with a kindly suggestion to lie down until the fever has passed.

But Thomson, a pilot who had narrowly missed active service during the war, meant business – and proved it, after convincing the solicitor, by building up the prestigious Caledonian Airways, later known as B-Cal, perhaps the outstanding success story of the British airline business.

Educated at Rutherglen Academy, the son of a railway shunter, Thomson joined the Fleet Air Arm at 17 then pursued a post-war career as a pilot with companies like British European Airways for the next 13 years.

For his ambition to start an airline he found a like-minded partner in a former BEA steward, John de la Haye, who was working for Eagle. They leased a plane from Sabena but had the worst possible start when that one and only machine crashed in West Africa, killing 100 people.

But Thomson survived to expand into the jet age with Boeing 707s and to buy over British United. The kind of solid Scot who impresses bankers, he took up routes where they were available, challenged the big national airlines and advocated two major companies for Britain instead of just British Airways.

He ran up against bureaucracy, however, and complained of preferential treatment for BA in matters of licensing, particularly in the lead-up to privatisation.

He had moved from the long-haul charter business to the scheduled sector, introduced a £99 return fare to New York, become a major player in the international scene from his base at Gatwick - and been given a knighthood in 1983.

But surprisingly, with a Thatcher Government so keen on the entrepreneur, he seemed out of favour in Whitehall and claimed they were determined that British Airways would take over B-Cal.

Much against his instincts, that is what happened in 1988. It was a sad and bitter end to the romantic story of Adam Thomson, the working lad from Glasgow's South Side who began with nothing but a dream and forged an aviation miracle.

The story of Willie Logan is of a different nature but hardly less colourful. His father, Duncan Logan, ran a small stone-cutting business at Muir of Ord, Ross-shire, but by the 1960s son Willie had taken them into major construction work, from road-making and hydro-electric dams to the pulp mill at Fort William.

As business grew, Logan Construction Company acquired its own light aircraft in 1962 and engaged Captain Duncan McIntosh, who flew with the RAF during the war, as the manager-cum-pilot of the small venture. In their Piper Aztec they could fly executives and key workers from site to site in the shortest time.

Willie Logan made headlines in 1963 when he flew into Dundee's airstrip bearing the successful tender to build the Tay Road Bridge - just 15 minutes before the submission deadline.

As Loganair became a name on Scottish lips, Willie acquired two more planes and was soon hiring them out, much sought after by the popular newspapers of the day when they needed aerial photographs. It had now become a business in its own right, with contracts to fly Littlewood football coupons around the country, computer cards from Glasgow to be processed by Ernie, the Premium Bond computer at Lytham St Anne's, and newspapers from Glasgow to Stornoway.

Loganair was then given permission to fly a limited number of passengers on that return flight from Stornoway.

In its expansion, the company was negotiating for new services in 1965 when tragedy struck twice. With his Highland background, Willie Logan was breaking a life-long rule about not working on Sundays when he went to supervise lifting operations on the Tay Road Bridge. A jib fell from the bridge, three men were killed and Willie himself was injured.

The second tragedy came a month later, in January 1966. Requiring to fly from Edinburgh to Inverness but finding his own planes engaged, he chartered a Piper Aztec from Strathallan Air Services. The plane crashed on the slopes of Craig Dunain on the approach to Inverness and Willie Logan was killed instantly.

Loganair became a limited company in 1966, its activities becoming less and less to do with the original construction company which, sadly, disappeared from the Scottish building scene after financial difficulties over its work on the Kingston Bridge in Glasgow.

By then Loganair was owned by the Royal Bank of Scotland and, in 1976, the fleet consisted of eight Islanders and six Trislanders, with an expanding range of routes. It was well established on the network of Scottish islands as well as on routes like Edinburgh-Manchester, previously run by British Airways.

When Captain McIntosh retired in 1982, already honoured with the OBE for his services to the people of the Highlands and Islands, he was succeeded as managing director by the finance director, Mr Scott Grier. A year later, the Royal Bank sold 75% of Loganair to British Midland, with Mr Grier taking up the remaining 25%.

In a further re-organisation in 1987, Loganair joined British Midland and Manx Airlines under the umbrella of Airlines of Britain Holdings plc, with Mr Grier selling off his stake but retaining the post of managing director.

With a staff reduced from 600 to 185, Loganair has now come to concentrate once more on Scotland, working a franchise arrangement with British Airways. Though the familiar name now takes second place in the livery, the company can pride itself in a brave contribution to the aviation story of Scotland.

Among its more eccentric features, it can claim to have the shortest route by fixed-wing aircraft in the world, as verified by the Guinness Book of Records.

The flight from the Orkney island of Westray to Papa Westray has a timetable duration of two minutes. With favourable headwind, the reality is just over a minute. And the record time for the journey, under Captain Andrew Alsop, was actually 58 seconds!

Adam Thomson

Willie Logan at Dundee in June 1963

In its contribution to the history of aviation, Scotland can take particular pride in its training of air crews. The names of Scone and Prestwick come to the fore as synonyms for flying instruction of the highest order, recognised by airlines throughout the world.

Few Scots passing those two airfields would have any idea that they have turned out pilots and engineers by the thousand – and continue to do so.

Though they developed in different ways, both found their origins in 1935. The Air Navigation Act having encouraged the building of municipal airports, Perth Town Council responded with the purchase of land from the Scone estate, creating its own aerodrome a few miles to the north-east of its boundary.

Perth has since reclaimed the name but it was for long known as Scone Aerodrome and stubbornly remains so in the public mind. More important, however, it attracted companies like Airwork Ltd, which offered flying training, and North-Eastern Airways, which began regular passenger services to Newcastle, Leeds and London, Aberdeen, Inverness and Renfrew.

Training of pilots, which began in 1936, was mainly for the Royal Air Force, the RAF Volunteer Reserve and University Air Squadrons and that continued until the 1950s when the emphasis changed to the civil sector.

Airwork Ltd had taken over the aerodrome in 1946 and Wing Commander Frank D Nugent became its principal and main influence for the next 31 years. In 1960 Airwork also acquired the engineering college at Hamble in Hampshire and moved it to Perth. With it came the name of Air Service Training, which then looked after the professional pilots while the Scottish Aero Club concentrated on those who fly as a pastime.

From the mid-1950s Perth was attracting overseas students and by 1972 had established an English Language School to support the Flying and Engineering Colleges. With English remaining the language of aviation, there were foreign students in need of basic tuition before they could qualify as pilots.

Through a substantial build-up, Perth has been called Britain's Air University, certainly one of the world's busiest and most prestigious centres of training.

Few airlines around the world are without the Scots influence and, in return, those students have brought a variety of sporting skills which show themselves from time to time in areas like the Perthshire cricket teams.

Among distinguished individuals who arrived as recruits at Perth was the young Neil Cameron, later to become Britain's Chief of the Defence Staff.

By contrast to Perth, the origins of flying instruction at Prestwick, recounted in another chapter, sprang from the pioneering work of David McIntyre and his

Formation flying over Air Service Training Ltd

colleague who later became the Duke of Hamilton.

Their early triumphs gave way to engineering and plane-building and their original company became part of what is known in the modern world as British Aerospace. Happily, in 1987, that national enterprise started its own British Aerospace Flying College and was soon turning out 200 graduates per year from Prestwick, fully-trained pilots for British Airways, Cathay Pacific and Gulf Air. With a fleet of 52 aircraft, they pride themselves in being a centre of excellence, giving cadets not only the full spinning and aerobatic training to enhance their skills but a knowledge of the business and commercial aspects of the airline industry as well.

Cadets live in the stately Adamton House, converted to give 257 rooms in the main building and annexe. Thus Prestwick, which started with a vision of training pilots, has come full circle more than half a century later.

A Piper PA-34 Seneca III from the BAe Flying College fleet. Students also fly the FFA Bravo and PA-28 Warrior II

Much of the flying training is now done in simulators like the Big Jet Systems Carrel illustrated here.

74

AVIATION MUSEUMS & COLLECTIONS

If this book has uncovered a story of aviation in Scotland which the reader knew little about, there is a pleasure in store for those who follow up the interest and seek out some of the aeroplanes for themselves.

The biggest collection is to be found in the Museum of Flight at East Fortune airfield, near Haddington, East Lothian, which is open every day from April till September.

Among the 40 exhibits to be seen, there is one of the first models mentioned in this book - the Hawk glider with which Scotland's Percy Pilcher was heading for fame, ahead of the Wright brothers of America, when his life was cut tragically short.

The Hawk was the only one of Pilcher's gliders to survive and it was secured for Scotland as far back as 1909. Another acquisition of that same year was a rare scale model of the Wright brothers' "Flyer" or Model A.

Other fascinating exhibits include the Weir autogyro, the sole survivor of that early involvement in building helicopters and autogyros of the Glasgow engineering company of G & J Weir of Cathcart.

You can see the Puss Moth as used by Amy Johnson and Jim Mollison in their

record-breaking flights of the 1930s, a Cygnet which was flown by Squadron Leader Guy Gibson, later of Dam Buster fame, a German Messerschmitt and one of the last Spitfires to be built during Second World War. There is a Vulcan bomber, a Sea Hawk and Scottish Aviation's Twin Pioneer – and an extensive collection of aero engines, dating from before 1914 up to one of the Olympus Jet engines from the Concorde prototype aircraft. Rockets also find a place in the East Fortune collection, with Blue Streak taking pride of place.

The Museum of Flight, which is part of the National Museums of Scotland, was opened in 1975 and has gradually extended the length of its season. An exhibition on the flight of Rudolf Hess in 1941 was a special feature during 1981, the same year in which East Fortune's collection was boosted by the arrival of five aircraft.

That purchase was some consolation for the sadness of the occasion at which they were bought. Those planes came from Britain's finest private collection at Strathallan, near Auchterarder in Perthshire, which had been started in 1969 by wealthy landowner Sir William Roberts and came to attract 20,000 people for air displays and up to 70,000 visitors a year. Unfortunately, it became too costly for a private individual to maintain.

East Fortune was certainly a suitable home for Strathallan planes and indeed for the whole museum. It had been a Royal Naval Air Station during the First World War and was used by the RAF in the Second War.

Historically, it had the added attraction of having been the departure point for the R34 airship which made the first east-west crossing of the Atlantic in 1919.

Scotland's other museums are small by comparison but are not without their

Inside one of the display hangers at the Museum of Flight

Duncan Simpson lands in the Hurricane during the 1976 Strathallan air show.

A Harvard prepares to take off from Strathallan airfield - July 1978.

interest. They range from Montrose, which can claim to have had Britain's first operational aerodrome during the First World War, to Dumfries, where the models on display include the Blue Peter Spitfire which crashed in the area in the Second World War and was buried nearby. The discovery and recovery work were filmed for the Blue Peter programme on television.

The efforts of one enthusiast, RAF veteran Richard Moss, has resulted in a commendable collection of memorabilia at Kirriemuir. Items range from bomber gun sights and mess cans to the diary kept by a German officer connected with the story of the Great Escape.

Richard Moss has devoted his life to building up the collection, which found much favour with thousands of visitors to the Glasgow Royal Concert Hall when it went on display during the 75th anniversary of the Royal Air Force in 1993.

There is an RAF section in the United Services Museum at Edinburgh Castle - and the 602 (City of Glasgow) Squadron has its own museum just off the Motorway on the way to Glasgow Airport.

This memorial to a band of famous men includes the Squadron silverware, a Rolls-Royce Merlin engine, uniforms and decorations, maps, reference books and paintings and the Battle of Britain Memorial Book. It was created by the staff and cadets of No. 2175 (Rolls-Royce) Squadron of the Air Training Corps.

A corner of the 602 Squadron Museum with photographs, memorabilia and uniforms

Aerial view of the Museum of Flight at East Fortune

MILITARY AVIATION IN SCOTLAND

Towards the end of the 20th century the Royal Air Force was operating from three main flying stations in Scotland - Leuchars (air defence), Kinloss (maritime patrol) and Lossiemouth (strike - and training for Tornadoes and Jaguars).

Squadrons have come and gone but the special affinity with No. 43 is its long association with Scotland. Re-born in 1969 at Leuchars, where it has continued to operate, the connection dates back to the original foundation which took place at Stirling in 1916. It became No. 43 Squadron of the Royal Flying Corps, retaining its identity in the new Royal Air Force which was founded in 1918. Disbanded a year later, it was back in business in 1925 and gained a high reputation in formation aerobatics in the 1930s. With biplane days over in 1939, it was equipped with Hurricanes in time for the Battle of Britain. Scrapped once more at the end of the war, it was alive at Leuchars in 1950, equipped with Hunters, saw service in Cyprus and Aden and was eventually joined by No 111 Squadron in looking after the northern sector of the United Kingdom's air defence region. It also took part in the Gulf conflict in 1991.

Though most of us know little of RAF structures or the planes which streak on northern skies, there are historic links to interest the layman.

In 1994, for example, Lossiemouth became home to No. 617 Squadron, better known to the world as the one which Wing Commander Guy Gibson led to immortality as the Dambusters of 1943, bursting the Möhne and Eder Dams in Germany with Barnes Wallis's bouncing bombs. Gibson gained the Victoria Cross. The squadron was lucky enough to be led by another legend of the skies, Wing Commander Leonard Cheshire, under whom it became expert at target marking .

A 617 Squadron Tornado GR1B taxies from its hardened shelter at Lossiemouth before take-off

In the 1990s Lossiemouth also housed No. XV Squadron, whose history included attacking Berlin with Stirlings in 1941. Its most famous Stirling was MacRobert's Reply, presented by Lady MacRobert of Douneside, Tarland, in Aberdeenshire, in memory of her sons (The story has a chapter to itself). Helicopters from Lossiemouth regularly distinguish themselves in rescue operations on land and at sea.

From Kinloss the Nimrod squadrons made their mark particularly during the Falklands War of 1982, flying to the South Atlantic and using air-to-air re-fuelling on their long-range patrols.

The only Royal Naval Air Station is at Prestwick, where No. 819 Naval Air Squadron moved with Sea King helicopters in 1971 as support for Clyde-based submarines and provides search and rescue facilities in the west of

Originally formed in the fields below Stirling Castle, a 43 Squadron Tornado F3 flies over its birthplace

A Nimrod MR2 from the Kinloss Maritime Wing overflying the Norwegian coast

A Jaguar GR1A of No. 16 (Reserve) Squadron coming to land at Lossiemouth

Vampire FB5s of No. 612 (County of Aberdeen) Squadron at Dyce in November 1952. Also seen are the Squadron's Meteor T7, Harvard T2 and Anson C19

During the 'Cold War' period the RAF's air defence squadrons regularly intercepted and turned away Soviet 'Bear' aircraft as they approached UK air space. This 43 Squadron Phantom is seen on such a mission in the 1970s

Hawker Harts of No. 603 (City of Edinburgh) Squadron based at Turnhouse over the Bass Rock in the mid 1930s

This Tornado F3 of 111 Squadron shadows a Russian Tupolev 'Bear' in friendlier times - it was going to the International Air Tattoo at Fairford in 1993

Firefly AS5, MB730 '210/AC', of 1830 Naval Air Squadron RNVR from Abbotsinch lands on HMS Illustrious during sea training in 1949 after which it won the Boyd Trophy

RAF Leuchars was the shore base for the Phantoms of No. 892 Naval Air Squadron when disembarked from HMS Ark Royal in the 1970s

Auster AOP6 of No. 666 (Scottish) Squadron R AuxAF seen at Turnhouse in January 1957 just before the unit disbanded

Scotland.

The auxiliary flying squadrons were disbanded in 1957, the stirring exploits of No. 602 and No. 603 finding their own place in this book. Others with a Scottish connection included No. 612 (County of Aberdeen), which was formed at Dyce in 1937 and took part in anti-submarine patrols during the war. No. 666 (Scottish) Army Co-operation Squadron was based at Scone from 1949 till 1957 and the Fleet Air Arm's No. 1830 was formed at Abbotsinch in 1947 as a fighter/anti-submarine squadron within the RNVR joined later by 1843 to form the Scottish Air division. No. 2 Maritime Headquarters Unit keeps the Royal Auxiliary Air Force flag flying, using the former town headquarters of 603 Squadron in Edinburgh.

Unthinkable in the 1980s, a Russian Air Force Su.27 'Flanker' arrives at Leuchars for the 1992 air show

A cadet pilot from the Universities of Glasgow & Strathclyde Air Squadron prepares for a flight in a Bulldog

Air Training Corps and CCF cadets are flown in Chipmunks of No. 12 Air Experience Flight based at Turnhouse and receive gliding instruction at Nos. 661, 662 & 663 Volunteer Gliding Schools at Kirknewton, Arbroath and Kinloss

A Hawker Hind of No. 602 (City of Glasgow) Squadron Auxiliary Air Force floodlit by Royal Artillery searchlights over Tait's Tower during the closing of the Empire Exhibition in October 1938

When Eric Gandar Dower came north in 1933 to open an airfield beside the Aberdeenshire village of Dyce, he could hardly have imagined that his modest patch would one day rank as the third busiest airport in Britain - and house the biggest heliport in the world.

The modern romance of what is now Aberdeen Airport (though the people of Dyce may have something to say about that) sprang entirely from the discovery of oil in the North Sea in the late 1960s and the establishment of Aberdeen as the oil capital of Europe.

With a steady stream of helicopters plying between land and offshore platforms, it is not hard to see how, in terms of total aircraft take-offs and landings, Aberdeen ranks above bigger passenger terminals like Glasgow.

The aircraft movement figures for 1993-94 tell the modern story. Heathrow was out in front with 413,400, Gatwick followed with 186,200 and Aberdeen came third with 116,300. Glasgow's total aircraft movement was 102,000.

From Gandar Dower's venture of the 1930s the progress into the post-war world was fairly predictable. In the early 1950s you could fly from Aberdeen to London by hops in a Pionair, better remembered as a Dakota. That was replaced by the Viscount and the Herald turboprop.

With rumours of North Sea activity – and the big oil companies playing their cards close to the chest – a Bristow Whirlwind helicopter appeared at Aberdeen Airport in the summer of 1967, a symbol of what lay ahead, even if it went largely unnoticed at the time.

Into the 1970s and the massive prospect of North Sea oil was a secret no more. As the black gold began to flow, the facilities at Dyce were far from adequate. A multi-million terminal, built on the opposite side of the airfield from Dyce village and now approached from the Aberdeen-Inverurie road, was opened by Princess Alexandra in 1977.

Aberdeen took on a cosmopolitan atmosphere which was reflected in its air traffic, with airlines taking up international routes and bringing on planes like the Boeing 757 and the Airbus 320.

But the statistics which give it such a high ranking in activity come largely from those helicopters which form the regular chain with the unimaginable on-goings out there in the North Sea community of oil rigs and platforms.

The three giants based at Aberdeen are British International, Bristow and Bond, whose fleets of rotor machines lend a constant air of urgency to the airport.

Bristow Helicopters, founded by the colourful Alan Bristow, started business in 1953 and, from its base at Redhill, Surrey, made that early move into the offshore scene in the mid the 1990s. In the 1990s it employs 600 people at

A 'Bristow Tiger' Super Puma prepares to land on BP's Forties Charlie platform. The Bristow fleet in Scotland boasts 23 AC.332L Super Pumas, 12 Sikorsky S-61Ns of which three are fitted with auto-pilot and auto-hover for search-and-rescue work, 2 Bell 214STs, 2 Bell 212s with auto-hover and 2 Sikorsky S-76A+s. The company operates from Aberdeen, Sumburgh, Stornoway, Unst and 'Safe Gothic' in the Brent Field

Aberdeen and on each weekday sends out around 60 flights to the rigs and platforms.

British International grew out of British European Airways, dating back to

1947 when it began as an experimental unit to develop rotor aircraft for passenger use, guided by Capt Jock Cameron. Moving into oil exploration, it established the Aberdeen base in 1967 and the Shetland one in 1971.

The company acquired its British International name in 1986 when it was sold to Mr Robert Maxwell, the media tycoon. After his mysterious death in 1991 there was a management buy-out and then a merger with the Canadian Helicopter Corporation.

Completing the big three, Bond Helicopters grew from the company founded in 1961 by an ex-RAF pilot, David Bond. In 1986 it moved the company headquarters to Aberdeen to consolidate the control off offshore operations and in 1993 acquired the Australian company of Lloyd Helicopters.

It shares the pride which these helicopter companies take in the part they have played in developing an industry which transformed the economy of Great Britain. Happily, the pioneering Gandar Dower lived to see it.

AS.332L Super Puma G–BKZE of British International Helicopters. This company has a fleet of 20 aircraft in Scotland comprising 10 Sikorsky S-61Ns, 7 AS.332L Super Pumas, 2 Sikorsky S-76s and one SA.365N2 Dauphin

Bond Helicopters SA.365N Dauphin about to land on a North Sea oil platform. Bond, now part of the world's largest helicopter group, operates 24 helicopters in Scotland ranging through 10 AS.332L Super Pumas, 7 SA.365 Dauphins, 4 Bolkow Bo.105 BDSs and 3 Sikorsky S-76Cs. The company also have two Beech Super King Airs which are used for Air Ambulance service.

The bitter political battle in which Prestwick lost its exclusive right as Scotland's North Atlantic gateway brought its own significant changes in the 1990s.

Major airlines like Air Canada and Northwest opted for a move to Glasgow and left Prestwick's spacious terminal building looking gauntly for another role, particularly as a freight bridge between North America and Europe.

Meanwhile Glasgow Airport, which had opened at Abbotsinch after the closure of Renfrew in 1966, welcomed the newcomers, added transatlantic flight to its already bustling domestic and European business and celebrated with a massive extension to the terminal.

Its Glasgow – London route was the busiest in Europe and the new-look airport building took on the appearance of a truly international concourse. The new prosperity was not without its problems however. With five airlines now flying to North America – British Airways, Northwest, American Airlines, Air Canada and United – there were going to be casualties of over-capacity. In 1994 Northwest pulled out altogether and American Airlines made drastic cuts in its Scottish presence.

The dramatic expansion of Aberdeen Airport coincided precisely with the rise of the North Sea oil industry while Edinburgh kept up its end with good connections not only to most big cities in the United Kingdom but to major European locations like Amsterdam, Brussels, Cologne, Dublin and Paris.

Looking back to the days of Percy Pilcher, who would have believed that within the first hundred years the Flying Scots could have created an aviation history so rich, adventurous and dramatic?

The terminal building at Glasow with the original international pier on which can be seen aircraft of Northwest, United and American Airlines. The new international pier and associated buildings opened in November 1994

A unique occasion at Glasgow Airport when three Concordes graced the terminal for the launch of the Glasgow–London Super Shuttle in 1983

British Airways use the Boeing 757 on the London Shuttle although Boeing 737s and 767s are also found on the route

KLM DC-3 PH-ASR at the opening of "Central Scotland Airport" at Grangemouth on 1 July 1939.

Loganair Islander G–AYXK "Captain Eric Starling FRAeS" at Dundee's Riverside Airport in the mid 1970s

Scandinavian Airlines System DC-6, SE–BDE "Alrik Viking" lands over the main A77 road at Prestwick in the early 1950s. The road vehicles were halted by traffic lights!

One of many Viscounts passing through Prestwick in the late 1960s on delivery to Capital Airlines in USA

British Eagle Viscount G–APZB comes in over the golf course to land at Renfrew in the early 1960s

Viscounts provided the backbone of BEA's domestic services in the 1970s two of which are seen with regional titles at Glasgow Airport in April 1972

British European Airways Vickers Vanguard, G–APEN, taxis for take off from Renfrew in the 1960s

Jimmy Logan, great Scottish variety artist and pilot during the 1960s in his Miles Gemini

KLM Lockheed L.1049 Super Constellation in 1956

Scottish Airlines DC-3 Dakota G–AMPP on the Isle of Man service

Pan American World Airlines Douglas DC-7C, N755PA "Clipper East Indian", in 1956

Caledonian Airways Douglas DC-7Cs in the new and old liveries

BOAC Boeing B-377 Stratocruiser, G–AKGK "Canopus", in 1956

Busier days – Transamerica DC-8, Laker DC-10 Skytrain, British Airways Boeing 747, Northwest B.747 plus two other aircraft in June 1980

BOAC Boeing 707, G–APFD, at night – May 1960

The short-lived Highland Express Airline's Boeing 747 passes a DC-10 of Northwest in September 1987

A British Airways Express Shorts SD 3-60, Manx Airlines ATP, Air UK Fokker 100, British Airways ATP and a Boeing 737 on the London Shuttle await their passengers in October 1994

Tridents were the mainstay of BEA's Glasgow-London services for many years and introduced the original Glasgow-LondonShuttle in 1975

Air 2000, using Boeing 757s, was the first airline to fly Trans-Atlantic services from Glasgow in 1989 heralding the wholesale transfer of flights from Prestwick in 1990.

Douglas DC-9 of British Midland Airways who also operate Boeing 737s on domestic and European flights

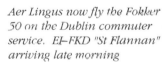

Aer Lingus now fly the Fokker 50 on the Dublin commuter service. EI-FKD "St Flannan" arriving late morning

British Airways inaugurated its Glasgow-New York service in August 1990 with Lockheed TriStars.

Britannia Airways used Boeing 737s on European holiday flights for many years

Boeing 767ERs of United Airlines fly daily to Washington

AIR CANADA & THE CANADIAN CONNECTION

The first regular air link between Scotland and Canada was established as early as 1943, growing out of the wartime connection when a Lancaster bomber was converted for mail, cargo and passengers.

From that wartime linking of Prestwick and Montreal came the peacetime service operated by the company we came to know as Air Canada. Prestwick continued to be the Scottish destination until 1990 when Air Canada was among those who decided to move their passenger services to Glasgow Airport. They also introduced the Boeing 767 which was complemented by the Boeing 747 with its seating capacity of 479.

Lockheed Super Constellations took over from the North Stars in 1954. During the 1960s it was possible to travel from Prestwick by Trans Canada Airlines to Halifax, Toronto, Montreal, Winnipeg and Vancouver

A USAAF C-54 transport takes off while a Trans Canada Airlines Lancaster, modified for passenger carrying, waits in front of the terminal at Prestwick in 1944. The Lancaster, CF–CMS, was the prototype conversion by Victory Aircraft of Montreal

After the transfer of passenger services to Glasgow in 1990, Air Canada continued to use Prestwick for freight until early 1994. One of its DC-8-73s, CF–TIQ, is seen landing

Canadair North Star at Prestwick in 1951. These aircraft entered service in 1947

Boeing 767-233ER in the airline's new livery is the type mainly used on services from Glasgow to Canada

David Huddleston from Giffnock graduated from the University of Glasgow where he learned to fly with the Air Squadron. He joined the Royal Canadian Air Force in the early 1960s and flew Lockheed Starfighters before commanding No. 434 Squadron. After commanding No. 1 Canadian Air Group in Europe he retired in the rank of Lieutenant General as Commander, Air Command, in 1993. His early enthusiasm was fired at the Prestwick Airport Aviation Group which was established in 1953 by the doyen of aircraft enthusiasts in the West, David Reid

One of the many Canadian Air Force Lockheed C-130 Hercules transports which regularly use Prestwick on their flights to Europe and Africa – September 1994